# DATE DUE

| | | | |
|---|---|---|---|
| | | | |
| | | | |
| | | | |
| | | | |
| | | | |
| | | | |
| | | | |
| | | | |
| | | | |
| | | | |
| | | | |
| | | | |
| | | | |
| | | | |
| | | | |
| | | | |

The Thirteen Colonies

# South Carolina

**Books in the Thirteen Colonies series include:**

Connecticut
Delaware
Georgia
Maryland
Massachusetts
New Hampshire
New Jersey
New York
North Carolina
Pennsylvania
Rhode Island
South Carolina
Virginia
The Thirteen Colonies: Primary Sources

The Thirteen Colonies

# South Carolina

Christina M. Girod

Lucent Books
10911 Technology Place, San Diego, California 92127

Library of Congress Cataloging-in-Publication Data

Girod, Christina M.
South Carolina / by Christina M. Girod.
p. cm. — (Thirteen colonies)
Includes bibliographical references and index.
Summary: Discusses the founding of South Carolina, daily life in its early years, its role in the American Revolution, its political and social ideology, and its achievement of statehood.
ISBN 1–56006–994–5 (alk. paper)
1. South Carolina—History—Colonial period, ca. 1600–1775—Juvenile literature. 2. South Carolina—History—1775–1865—Juvenile literature. [1. South Carolina—History—Colonial period, ca. 1600–1775. 2. South Carolina—History—1775–1865.] I. Title. II. Thirteen colonies (Lucent Books)
F272 .G53 2002
974.7'02—dc21

2001003775


an imprint of The Gale Group
10911 Technology Place, San Diego, California 92127



Printed in the U.S.A.

# Contents

# Foreword

The story of the thirteen English colonies that became the United States of America is one of startling diversity, conflict, and cultural evolution. Today, it is easy to assume that the colonists were of one mind when fighting for independence from England and afterwards when the national government was created. However, the American colonies had to overcome a vast reservoir of distrust rooted in the broad geographical, economic, and social differences that separated them. Even the size of the colonies contributed to the conflict; the smaller states feared domination by the larger ones.

These sectional differences stemmed from the colonies' earliest days. The northern colonies were more populous and their economies were more diverse, being based on both agriculture and manufacturing. The southern colonies, however, were dependent on agriculture—in most cases, the export of only one or two staple crops. These economic differences led to disagreements over things such as the trade embargo the Continental Congress imposed against England during the war. The southern colonies wanted their staple crops to be exempt from the embargo because their economies would have collapsed if they could not trade with England, which in some cases was the sole importer. A compromise was eventually made and the southern colonies were allowed to keep trading some exports.

In addition to clashing over economic issues, often the colonies did not see eye to eye on basic political philosophy. For example, Connecticut leaders held that education was the route to greater political liberty, believing that knowledgeable citizens would not allow themselves to be stripped of basic freedoms and rights. South Carolinians, on the other hand, thought that the protection of personal property and economic independence was the basic foundation of freedom. In light of such profound differences it is amazing that the colonies were able to unite in the fight for independence and then later under a strong national government.

Why, then, did the colonies unite? When the Revolutionary War began the colonies set aside their differences and banded together because they shared a common goal—gaining political freedom from what they considered a tyrannical monarchy—that could be more easily attained if they cooperated with each other. However, after the war ended, the states abandoned unity and once again pursued sectional interests, functioning as little nations in a weak confederacy. The congress of this confederacy, which was bound by the Articles of Confederation, had virtually no authority over the individual states. Much bickering ensued—the individual states refused to pay their war debts to the national government, the nation was sinking further into an economic depression, and there was nothing the national government could do. Political leaders realized that the nation was in jeopardy of falling apart. They were also aware that European nations such as England, France, and Spain were all watching the new country, ready to conquer it at the first opportunity. Thus the states came together at the Constitutional Convention in order to create a system of government that would be both strong enough to protect them from invasion and yet nonthreatening to state interests and individual liberties.

The Thirteen Colonies series affords the reader a thorough understanding of how the development of the individual colonies helped create the United States. The series examines the early history of each colony's geographical region, the founding and first years of each colony, daily life in the colonies, and each colony's role in the American Revolution. Emphasis is given to the political, economic, and social uniqueness of each colony. Both primary and secondary quotes enliven the text, and sidebars highlight personalities, legends, and personal stories. Each volume ends with a chapter on how the colony dealt with changes after the war and its role in developing the U.S. Constitution and the new nation. Together, the books in this series convey a remarkable story—how thirteen fiercely independent colonies came together in an unprecedented political experiment that not only succeeded, but endures to this day.

Introduction

# South Carolina's Wealth

In colonial times South Carolina was known as a land of great opportunity—a place where anyone of any class or birthright could rise to a place of prominence, wealth, and power within the local society. For many this was definitely the case, but for others the dream remained elusive. Nevertheless, for more than a century, South Carolina continued to be home to the largest proportion of wealthy families anywhere in the North American colonies.

This wealth was acquired at great expense to the people who settled the land. The colonists who first came to South Carolina faced attacks from Native Americans, extremes of weather, hard work, and frequent disease epidemics. Nowhere in all the colonies was the mortality rate as high as it was in South Carolina.

Africans who were forced to labor in the sweltering heat of the Carolina swamps paid an even higher price. Most were not there by choice, having been kidnapped from their homeland and forced into a life of slavery in a foreign land. Over time the institution of slavery became entrenched in the society and economy of the region, the African slaves stripped of their humanity to justify the existence of a system deemed necessary for the material prosperity of the colony.

Despite the existence of slavery, South Carolina's way of life—the pursuit of wealth and the opportunity to rise from poverty and low circumstances to a position of power—exemplifies much of the American spirit today. At the Constitutional Convention of 1787, it was a South Carolinian who best described what it meant to be American. In a speech, delegate Charles Pinckney said:

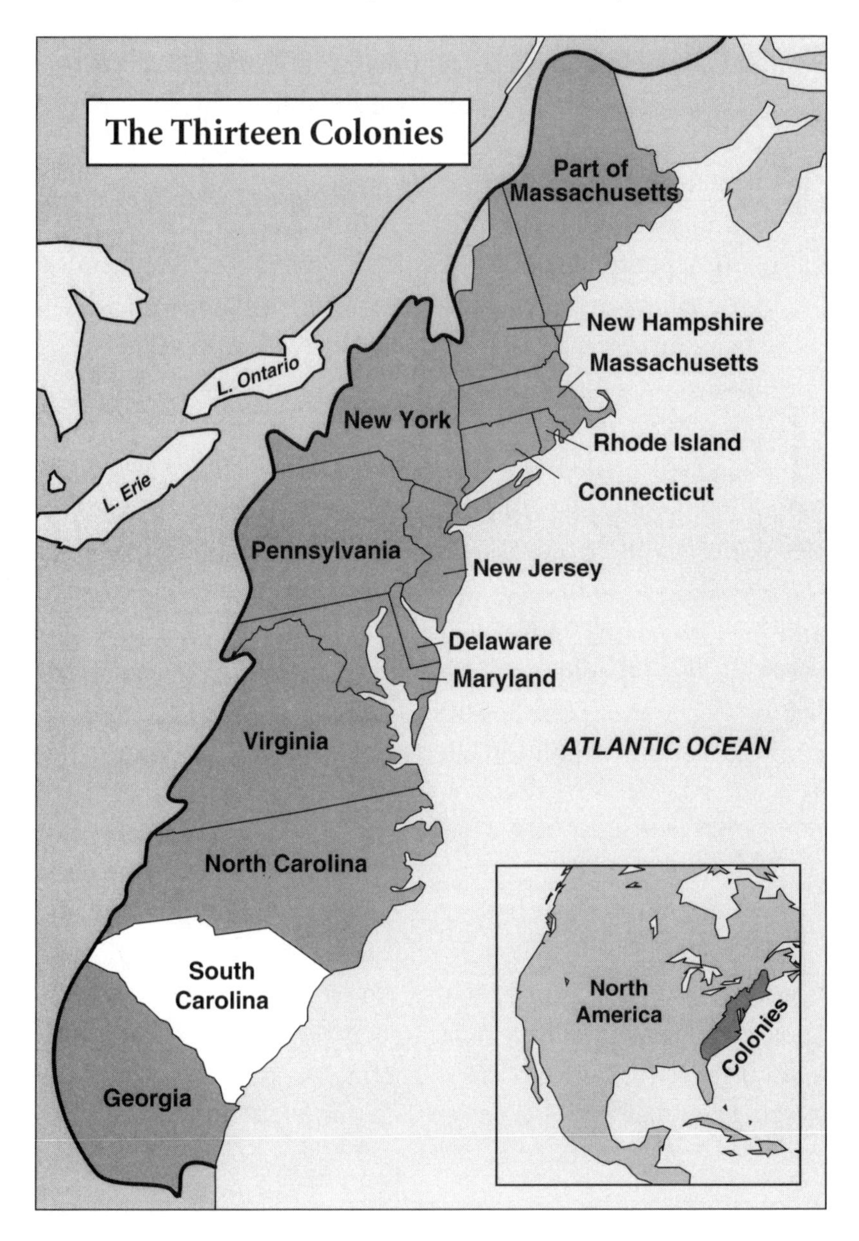

> [The American people are] the most singular of any we are acquainted with. . . . [They display] fewer distinctions of fortune and less of rank, than among the inhabitants of any other nation. . . . Our true situation appears to me to be this—a new extensive country containing within itself the materials for forming a government capable of extending to its citizens all the blessings of civil and religious liberty [and] capable of making them happy at home. . . . Every member of the society almost, will enjoy an equal power of arriving at the supreme offices. . . . None will be excluded by birth and few by fortune, from voting. . . . The whole community will enjoy in the fullest sense that kind of political liberty which consists in the power the members of the states reserve to themselves, of arriving at the public offices, or at least, of having votes in the nomination of those who fill them.[1]

Although his statement extended only to white males at the time, it held the potential that over the two centuries that followed, the Revolution would come closer and closer to fulfillment. In time slavery would be abolished, women would gain the right to vote, and laws would be implemented to protect the civil rights of everyone, regardless of race, creed, or gender. Of course, prejudices still exist in society, but South Carolina is closer to the ideal of complete social and political liberty today than ever before.

Chapter One

# Before the Colony: The Struggle to Settle Carolina

In the earliest days of recorded history, the region known today as the state of South Carolina was a bitter fighting ground between various peoples and nations. Some were fighting for economic reasons and others because it was their homeland. Although at first the battle was contained mainly between the natives, the Spanish, and the French, the English came into the fray later but proved the most successful in establishing settlements in the region.

The English were successful because they happened to have better managers and the financial support of their government. They were also fortunate to have the almost unswerving loyalty of one of the larger and more powerful Native American tribes of the region.

## Indigenous People of South Carolina

For thousands of years before the coming of Europeans, several groups of Native Americans inhabited the region of South Carolina. To the west the Cherokee lived in the southern Appalachian Mountains, while the Yamasee, Cusabo, and Coosa—Muskogean-speaking tribes—lived along the Savannah River in the south coastal regions. Next to the Cherokee, the largest group in South Carolina was the Catawba, a Siouan-speaking tribe that lived in the central and northeastern portions of the state.

The Catawba (meaning "river people"), along with a sister tribe called the Iswa, numbered about ten thousand people before contact with Europeans. However, by the time the English established their colony in South Carolina, war, disease, and alcohol had reduced the Catawba and Iswa population to four hundred.

The Catawba lived very much like other tribes in the southeastern part of North America. They resided in six villages containing circular, bark-covered houses surrounding a central temple structure that was used for social gatherings, important meetings, and spiritual ceremonies. Surrounding the village were immense crops of corn, beans, and squash, which the men planted and harvested and the women cared for during the growing season. Their diet was supplemented with meat from hunting—especially the white-tailed deer—and with fish and small game. A clerk on board an English vessel that arrived in South Carolina in 1680 described them as follows: "They are excellent hunters, their weapons the bow and arrow, made of reed, pointed with sharp stones, or fish bones; their clothing skins of the bear or deer, the skin dressed after their country fashion."[2] The women also gathered fruits, nuts, and berries in the woods.

Besides farming and hunting, the Catawba made war a major part of their lifestyle. The Catawba were reputed to be among the fiercest of warriors and had an appearance that drove fear into their enemies. A warrior pulled his long, black hair into a ponytail, accentuating his forehead, which had been flattened at birth with a board—the custom with all Catawba male infants—and then painted a black circle around one eye and a white circle around the other, with the rest of the face painted entirely black.

The Catawba were constantly at war with the Cherokee and other neighboring tribes, but after the Shawnee arrived in 1660, the fighting became even more intense. The Shawnee were driven from their homeland in the north by the Iroquois and were allowed by the Cherokee to settle in the area between them and the Catawba to act as a military buffer. However, the presence of the Shawnee resulted in occasional raids by the Seneca from the north, who sometimes mistakenly attacked other tribes, including the Catawba.

With so many enemies battling in the region now, the Catawba recognized the need for a strong ally. They found this ally in the English colonists who settled in South Carolina after 1670. This alliance also resulted in the Catawba being adequately stocked with guns and ammunition, allowing them to engage in highly successful raids against their enemies.

The Catawba were a major reason why the English were able to successfully settle South Carolina. Through the years of the American Revolution, the Catawba consistently fought on the side of the colonists, against other tribes, the French, and later the British army. Only once did the Catawba take up arms against the colonists, during the Yamasee War in 1715. However, long before they allied themselves with the English, the Catawba encountered the French and the Spanish, who repeatedly attempted to settle the coast of South Carolina.

The only time the Catawba tribe fought against the colonists was during the Yamasee War in 1715.

## Early Spanish Exploration

Soon after early explorers discovered North America—which they called the New World—several European nations began vying for control of the new land. Spain quickly sent explorers to the Gulf of Mexico to lay claim to the region. In its first attempt at settlement in South Carolina, Spain approved six ships loaded with five hundred

# The Lady of Cofitachequi

*In 1540 Spanish explorer Hernando de Soto and his caravan of six hundred soldiers and slaves began a journey through the southeastern part of North America, including the region that is present-day South Carolina.*

*While making his way up the Wateree River, de Soto came across the town of Cofitachequi. Here he was graciously greeted by the female leader of the town—today she is often referred to as the Lady of Cofitachequi. From the time of de Soto's arrival when the Lady took a strand of her own pearls and placed them over his head, he and his men were treated like honored guests.*

*The Lady, however, was keeping a close eye on her guests, well aware of the slavery, disease, and destruction that often came with the Spaniards' visits. After two weeks in Cofitachequi, de Soto decided to move on; the Gentleman of Elvas, quoted in Walter Edgar's book* South Carolina: A History, *wrote an account of how the Spaniards took their leave:*

> On the third day of May, the Governor [de Soto] set out from Cutifachiqui [Cofitachequi]; and, it being discovered that the wish of the Cacica [the Lady] was to leave the Christians, if she could ... because of the outrages committed upon the inhabitants ... the Governor ordered that she should be placed under guard and took her with him. This treatment ... was not a proper return for the hospitable welcome he had received.

*Apparently de Soto thought the Lady would serve as a guide and a preventative against attack by other Indians. Soon, however, the Lady slipped away from the Spaniards and returned to her people in Cofitachequi.*

settlers led by Lucas Vásquez de Ayllón in 1526. Soon after they arrived, the supply ship sank, leaving the settlers, men, and women from the island of Hispaniola in the Caribbean, stranded without food or tools. Panicked, the settlers decided to abandon the site. Before they could leave, local Indians attacked them, killing 350 people. The survivors managed to sail back to Hispaniola.

After the failure of Ayllón's settlement, Spain waited more than thirty years before making another attempt to settle the South Carolina coast. By the 1550s, the Spanish were bringing back to Spain tremendous treasures of gold and silver from Mexico and South America. However, their loaded galleons were frequently the target of attacks by English and French pirates who were either employed by their governments or using their privateers for personal gain.

As a result, the Spanish began to look for a place to man a defense post for their treasure galleons along the southern Atlantic coast of North America. In 1557 the Spanish entered what is now called Port Royal Sound and claimed the land for Spain, naming the site Santa Elena. Spain's several attempts to settle Santa Elena were mostly unsuccessful because the Spanish government was more interested in continuing to find gold and other valuables rather than in financing settlements. One English pirate commented that the Spanish garrison at Santa Elena served "for no other purpose, than to keep all other nations from inhabiting any part"[3] of the region. This Spain accomplished until 1561, when royal authorities decided the cost of settling the region was too high and abandoned plans to develop the area.

## French Attempts at Settlement

At the same time the Spanish were laying claim to the South Carolina region, the French were also attempting to settle there. In 1524 Giovanni da Verrazano, a Florentine sailing for France, explored the southern coast of North America as a possible site for a colony for religious refugees should France become embroiled in a civil war. At the time, political tension existed in France between Protestants—called Huguenots—and Catholics, which threatened to explode into violence.

In 1524, Giovanni da Verrazano sailed along the southern coast of North America in search of potential French colony sites.

For nearly forty years peace remained, however, and the colony did not materialize. In 1562 a Frenchman named Jean Ribault convinced the French government to support a settlement on the South Carolina coast. Ribault took only a few men and sailed to the now-abandoned site of Santa Elena, which he renamed Port Royal, the name it holds today. At Port Royal Ribault erected a small fort, Charlesfort, which he left with several volunteers to defend while he returned to France to collect more supplies and recruit settlers. René Laudonnière recounted Ribault's settlement of Port Royal in his book *A Notable Historie Containing Four Voyages Made by Certain French Captaines:*

> We . . . sailed three leagues toward the West, where we discovered . . . a little island, separated from the firm land, where we went on shore; and by commandment of the captain, because it was exceedingly fair and pleasant, there we planted the pillar upon a hillock open round about to view. . . . Whereupon John [Ribault], being as glad as might be to see his men so well willing, determined the next day to search the most fit and convenient place to be inhabited. . . . Which done . . . he found a very open place . . . where he went on land, and seeing the place fit to build a fortress in, and commodious for them that were willing to plant there, he resolved . . . the fort to be made in length about sixteen fathoms, and thirteen in breadth, with flanks. . . . We worked so diligently, that in a short space the fort was made in some sort defensible, in which meantime John Ribault

> caused victuals and warlike ammunition to be brought for the defense of the place. . . . This being done, we sailed toward the North, and then we named this river Port Royal, because of the largeness and excellent fairness of the same.[4]

Unfortunately, during Ribault's absence, war had broken out between the Catholics and the Protestants in France. With the country embroiled in civil war, Ribault could find no support for his New World venture. He instead turned to England, which was aiding the Huguenots, thinking he could find support there. For unknown reasons, however, the English grew suspicious of his intentions and imprisoned him. It was not until 1564, after the war in France ended and Ribault was freed, that he was able to gather the needed supplies for the settlement.

Ribault, however, returned to Port Royal to find it abandoned. In his absence, the men left behind had "entered into partialities and dissensions [over the cruel treatment they received from the captain]. . . . They fell into a mutiny . . . [and] they put him [the captain] to death."[5] They chose a new leader and decided to abandon Charlesfort, with their food and supplies running dangerously low. Few reached France, and those that did had resorted to cannibalism before being saved by an English vessel. As a result, Ribault concentrated his efforts a little farther south, closer to Spanish Florida, where he built Fort Caroline.

## The Spanish Return

In the meantime, Spain renewed its interest in settling North America, and soldiers constructed a large fort at St. Augustine in 1565. From this stronghold, the Spanish attacked the French garrison at Fort Caroline and destroyed it. They hunted down Ribault and his men and executed them, ending the brief era of French attempts to settle the South Carolina coast.

With the French removed, the Spanish returned to the site of Santa Elena, rebuilding their fort and erecting a mission. The town and fort served as the capital of La Florida, as Spanish territory in North America was called. For a time the mission thrived as the

Spanish soldiers attack and kill Jean Ribault and his men, ending French attempts to settle the coast of South Carolina.

center of a small farming community, which by October 1569 had grown to 327 men, women, and children. Santa Elena's inhabitants worked as soldiers, farmers, or artisans, although most of the town's economy was maintained by trade with Indians because crops in the frequently flooded coastal lowland were poor.

Despite its growth, the town was plagued by disease and food shortages, as one colonist complained: "[The settlers were] driven by hunger to the coast with their wives and children, to eat shellfish and oysters, for if they had not done so, they would have perished from hunger."[6] Faced with the threat of starvation, many Spanish colonists raided nearby Indian villages for food. Santa Elena was already vulnerable to Indian attacks because unlike the Florida tribes, the Catawba and other peoples in the area rejected European ways and religious beliefs. As a result, by the mid-1570s Indian attacks had increased.

In 1576 the incompetence of despotic Spanish leaders in Santa Elena brought tensions with the natives to a head. That year Spanish authorities murdered three Indian leaders and attacked several villages. In reprisal, a majority of the native peoples in the area united and launched a massive attack on Santa Elena. Most of the soldiers were killed defending the town, and the residents fled to the fort for safety. For a while the settlers remained trapped in the fort, but they managed to escape to the sea and traveled to St. Augustine or Cuba. The natives then burned the town and fort and proceeded to destroy every Spanish settlement along the Atlantic coast except for St. Augustine.

Undaunted, the following year the Spanish rebuilt a new fort at Santa Elena, named San Marcos. Although the town of Santa Elena was also rebuilt, it no longer served as La Florida's capital, which had been moved to St. Augustine. By the early 1580s, the town was once again growing. Although farmers had more success with crops farther inland, continued tensions with the Indians made extensive crop cultivation difficult. Santa Elena's rebirth, however, was soon cut short.

In 1586 Sir Francis Drake, sailing for Great Britain, led a military force against the Spanish, destroying St. Augustine. With their military stronghold laid waste, the Spanish were forced to abandon their more vulnerable outposts, including Santa Elena. Despite protests the settlers were ordered to burn their homes and the fort and abandon the town. Although the Spanish eventually rebuilt St. Augustine, they never returned to Santa Elena, leaving the region open to settlement by other nations.

The fort at San Marcos (as it stands today) was built after Native Americans destroyed the fort at Santa Elena.

## English Interest in the Southern Atlantic Coast Grows

England was the latecomer in the race to settle the southern Atlantic coast for several reasons. One was that domestic issues during the 1500s took precedence over any grand ideas for colonizing the New World. For the most part, England looked at the region primarily as a vantage point from which to harass its enemies, preying on treasure galleons en route to Spain. Then in 1587 war between Spain and England broke out, and for more than a decade any thoughts of imperial colonization were forgotten.

Finally, when peace was declared in 1604 between England and Spain, the English government began to concentrate on colonizing the New World. King James I, however, was wary of settling too close to Spanish Florida and decided to establish colonies in the more northern region that became New England.

The first hint of English interest in settling the southern Atlantic coast came in 1629 with the Heath grant, a piece of property granted, or given, to Sir Robert Heath, an attorney general of England, by James's successor, King Charles I. The grant stretched from Virginia to Spanish Florida and west all the way to the Pacific

Ocean. The land tract from this grant was named "Carolana" in honor of Charles I. This grant gave Heath a vast array of powers:

> Know that we . . . do erect and incorporate them [the boundaries] into a province and name the same Carolana. . . .We . . . do give power to the said Sir Robert . . . to form, make and enact and publish . . . what laws soever may concern the public state of the said province, or the private profit of all according to the wholesome directions of and with the counsel, assent and approbation of the freeholders of the same province. . . . Furthermore, lest the way to honours . . . may seem to be . . . altogether barred up to men honestly born and who are willing to undertake this present expedition and are desirous in so remote and far distant a region to deserve well of . . . our Kingdom in peace and war . . . we . . . give full and free power to . . . Sir Robert Heath . . . to confer favours, graces, and honours upon those well deserving citizens . . . and the same with whatever titles and dignities . . . to adorn at his pleasure.[7]

For a while Heath entertained the idea of colonizing the area with Huguenots, French Protestants who had fled to England to avoid religious persecution. While several plans were drawn up, the expedition never materialized, and Heath gradually lost interest in the idea during the early 1630s. He eventually gave his title to the grant to Henry, Lord Maltravers.

Lord Maltravers made several failed attempts to settle the region. The problem was mainly that the settlements in Virginia, Massachusetts, and Maryland offered too much competition for colonists and supplies. Thus a

King Charles I (pictured) granted "Carolana," a stretch of land named in honor of himself, to Sir Robert Heath in 1629.

successful expedition was even beyond the resources of a wealthy nobleman.

Interest in colonization waned even more after the outbreak of a civil war in England in the 1640s. Opponents of the monarchy, many of whom were Puritans, dethroned King Charles in 1649 and

## Disease in Colonial Times

Disease was more prevalent in colonial South Carolina than anywhere else in the colonies. Between 1670 and 1775 there were fifty-nine major epidemics in the colony, including eighteen of yellow fever, nine of smallpox, and four of influenza. Malaria and typhus were also common. These diseases were carried by Europeans and Africans, and also by pests such as the mosquito, the black rat, and the cockroach, all of which thrived in South Carolina's semitropical climate.

Malaria was troublesome because it was often fatal to children and pregnant women. Moreover, although most adults survived the disease, malaria weakened the immune system, making survivors more susceptible to other conditions such as whooping cough, measles, and dysentery. Epidemics of malaria, typhus, and yellow fever were more common in the low country because people lived near their rice fields in the swamps. No one knew at that time that the swamps were breeding grounds for mosquitoes.

The mortality rate from disease in South Carolina was extraordinary. For children in the low country it was sometimes as high as 80 percent. Of the one hundred children baptized in Christ Church Parish, eighty-six of them died before the age of twenty. In St. John's Berkeley Parish, one-third of those who reached age twenty never lived to the age of forty. Sometimes whole families were wiped out. In Prince William Parish, the rector, his wife, and all five of his children were "cut off by the Endemic Fever that rages here, and not one now left," as one colonist was quoted by historian Walter Edgar in his book *South Carolina: A History*. The three sons of Richard and Mary Savage all died within ten days of each other. The boys were just three, five, and seven. Nevertheless, many settlers persisted in living in South Carolina even at the almost certain risk of premature death.

set up a republican form of government that lasted for eleven years. During this period, funds for British settlements in North America tended to be directed to the colonies in New England rather than for the establishment of new ones. It was not until 1660 when the monarchy was restored with the coronation of Charles's son as King Charles II that interest in new colonies for England in the New World arose.

★★★★★

# Chapter Two

# Founding the Colony

With the renewed interest of the English Crown in expanding the British Empire, the region of South Carolina finally developed a few permanent—and successful—settlements. The first Carolina settlements were located within the boundaries of modern North Carolina, but by 1670 South Carolina was also inhabited by English settlers. These settlers were experienced colonists from other remote regions and soon developed their own political and social structures based primarily on the economic system of the region. These structures eventually brought the colonists into conflict with the government of Carolina—a group of eight proprietors.

## The Charters of Carolina

Charles II owed a great deal to the noblemen who had supported the idea of a British monarchy during years of Puritan rule, and who ultimately helped him gain the throne. As thanks to eight of these men, he granted them a charter to a tract of land that was included in part of the old Heath grant, and changed the name from Carolana to Carolina. This charter, drawn up in 1663, met with some complaints by Heath's successors. However, Charles II disposed of these claims by annulling the Heath grant.

With legal obstructions cleared, Charles then granted these eight noblemen another charter in 1665, which was identical to the first, except that the boundaries of Carolina were expanded to stretch from Albemarle, Virginia, in the north to St. Augustine, Florida, in the south. By stretching the southern boundary to the Spanish garrison, Charles II hoped to put pressure on Spain.

The men to whom the charter was granted were the lords proprietors of the colony, with power to govern Carolina as they saw fit. The charter stated:

> We [the British government] . . . do grant full and absolute power . . . to them [the proprietors] . . . for the good and happy government of the said whole province or territory, full power and authority to erect, constitute and make several counties . . . and also to ordain, make and enact . . . any laws and constitutions whatsoever, either appertaining to the public state of the said province or territory . . . with the advice, assent and approbation of the freemen of the said province.[8]

The proprietors also had the authority to grant land to colonists, to construct military fortifications and train men to defend them, and to establish Anglican churches for the proliferation of the Church of England in Carolina. Their power went so far as to allow them to declare martial law in case of mutiny or rebellion among the colonists.

King Charles II (pictured) annulled Robert Heath's grant and issued land in Carolina to eight of his noblemen.

Despite their sweeping authority, in practice the proprietors were quite liberal in their governance of Carolina.

They were generous in granting land to prospective settlers and allowed a high degree of self-government in the colony. One reason for this liberality was that the proprietors needed a way to attract settlers to the region—and free land was what attracted most people. They also recognized the need for experienced colonists who could more readily adapt to the difficulties of frontier life. Therefore it was to people in already established English colonies in North America and the Caribbean that the proprietors advertised their free land in Carolina.

## The First English Settlements in Carolina

The first people to venture into Carolina were Puritans from Massachusetts. They settled on the Cape Fear River in early 1663 but suddenly abandoned the site only a few months later. All that they left behind was a sign cursing the land as evil.

The proprietors hurriedly buried the story of the cursed site without bothering to discover its origins and set about attracting a new group to settle Carolina. In 1665 another group of New Englanders settled at Cape Fear, and these were soon joined by a group from the English colony on Barbados. Although it lasted longer than the first settlement, it too had vanished by 1667 because

Puritans from Massachusetts were the first people to settle in Carolina.

of problems with the local Indians, consistently stormy weather in the area, and the destruction of a supply ship, which left them short of food and tools.

This latter settlement did have one lasting effect on the future of Carolina. On separate occasions the colonists sent two men to explore the Carolina coast for other suitable settlement sites. One of these men left behind a companion, Dr. Henry Woodward, who wanted to acquaint himself with the Carolina natives. Woodward had many experiences on the Carolina frontier, including being captured by the Spanish and imprisoned at St. Augustine, later to be rescued by an English pirate who was shipwrecked on the Atlantic coast.

Woodward, who helped found the first permanent settlement in Carolina at Albemarle Point in 1670, became quite popular with the local natives and was so adept at persuading them to ally with the English that the Spanish came to resent him personally. A fellow Briton, Robert Sanford, who had been sent out to explore the Carolina coast by the Cape Fear settlers, described Woodward's effect on the Indians in 1666:

> I called the Cassique [chief] and another old man and their wives And in sight and heareing of the whole Towne, delivered Woodward into their charge. . . . They received him with such Testimonys of Joy and thankfullnes as hughely confirmed to me their great desire of our friendship and society. The Cassique placed Woodward by him uppon the Throne and after lead him forth and shewed him a large field of Maiz [corn] [which he] told him should bee his, and then hee brought him the Sister of the Indian that I had with mee telling him that shee should tend him and dresse his victualls [prepare food for a meal].[9]

Woodward played a role in the ability of the English to gain the friendship of the local natives, allowing the settlement of 1670 to flourish.

## The Founding of Charles Town

In 1669 the proprietors put together and financed another group of settlers—only this time they would settle in the southern part of Carolina, near Port Royal. Three ships, named *Carolina*, *Port Royal*, and *Albemarle*, were outfitted with food, seeds, ammunition, tools, and other provisions. En route from England the ships were to stop at Barbados for passengers who wanted to go to Carolina. The proprietors agreed to allow anyone passage who would agree to pay them, either on the spot, in cash, or within two years with tobacco, cotton, or ginger.

The ships, under the command of Captain Joseph West, reached Barbados in October 1669 with a score of English colonists. Here he recruited more colonists from the planters on the island, bringing the total of colonists up to about 130. Many were eager for the new opportunity in Carolina because the island of Barbados had become increasingly crowded with plantations. The proprietors sought settlers from Barbados because they were already experienced at colonial frontier life, and the proprietors believed they could avoid the difficult period of adjustment during which new settlements frequently failed because of high mortality rates.

Unfortunately, however, this new expedition began to founder before it even reached the New World. The Caribbean autumn brought violent storms to Barbados, wrecking the *Albemarle*. Later the *Port Royal* was shipwrecked in the Bahamas. This left only the *Carolina* and a Barbadian replacement ship in the fleet bound for Carolina. Finally, the *Carolina* arrived at Port Royal in March 1670. The Barbadian ship went off course and did not arrive until May.

Captain West and the colonists did not stay in Port Royal, however. Instead they chose a site twenty-five miles inland on the western side of the Ashley River. Although the local natives made offers of friendship, out of their loyalty to Woodward, the colonists felt safer within a tight palisade of walls. Within this palisade they built a small town, which they named Charles Town in honor of the king of England. Keeping the community tight meant that initially farms had

Settlers of Charles Town chop wood near the Ashley River.

to be small, and for the first couple of years the colonists cultivated only ten-acre land plots, although they were entitled to much more.

## Early Political Divisions

Almost immediately the fledgling community of Charles Town was beset by political conflict. The conflict developed over whether Joseph West or Sir John Yeamans, a former Barbadian planter and politician, had the right to act as governor. The first governor, William Sayle, a Barbadian leader who was close to eighty when he accepted the governorship of Carolina, died after only a year in office. Although Sayle named West, the former captain of the founding expedition, as his successor, Yeamans used his own seniority as a nobleman to challenge the appointment. Yeamans petitioned the lords proprietors on behalf of his position. Shortly thereafter, Yeamans's commission from the proprietors arrived and he officially became governor.

Yeamans soon proved to be a man who operated for self-interests rather than the interests of the colony. During these early years when food was scarce, Yeamans sold his produce in Barbados rather than to the Carolinians, simply because he could get a higher price for it there. The colonists became disenchanted with him as governor, and West claimed that the public was "saying Sir John intended to make this a Cape Fear settlement [implying he meant to destroy it]."[10] By 1674 the proprietors had grown dissatisfied with Yeamans and replaced him with West, who served competently for eight years.

## Relocation and Growth of Charles Town

Throughout the 1670s, the colonists and Indians remained on peaceful terms, but by 1680 tensions between them had grown as the population of Charles Town increased. That year the colonists decided to move the site of Charles Town from Albemarle Point to the lowland region at a place called Oyster Point (the point of land where the Ashley and Cooper Rivers converged), which had an excellent port from which to ship the commodities produced in Carolina. This new site became what is now Charleston, South Carolina; the original site was called Old Town for a while and then became Kiawah. A colonist who identified himself only as "T. A." described Charles Town in 1682:

> The place called Charles Town, by an express order from the Lords Proprietors of Carolina in the year 1680, their ordnance and ammunition being removed thither from Old Charles Town . . . both for its strength [militarily] and

Colonists load their belongings into boats for the move to Oyster Point.

commerce. It is very commodiously [spaciously] situated from many other navigable rivers that lie near it on which the planters are seated. . . . The planters may bring their commodities to the town as to the common market . . . both for trade and shipping. The town is regularly laid out into large . . . streets . . . [with] convenient places for building a

## The Perils of Coming to Colonial South Carolina

*In 1701 Edward and Elizabeth Hyrne arrived in Charles Town, South Carolina, with little money to invest in their new life. Edward wrote to his brother-in-law in England about the troubles they were having securing supplies and a livelihood. This excerpt is from H. Roy Merrens's book,* The Colonial South Carolina Scene:

> Captain Flavel has paid me all the money . . . the whole amount . . . is 175.15.0 [175 British pounds, 15 shillings] of which I was above 100 [pounds] in debt when the ship arriv'd . . . for rent, doctors, victuals, and other necessaries: all which sum I have now paid and the remainder . . . is all I have to begin the world with here. . . . I have likewise found credit for a brave plantation, which I bought . . . for 1,000 Carolina-money . . . [and] I think I have made a very good bargain. . . . If [I] had a competent number of hands, I doubt not but cou'd raise the money off the plantation by that time it becomes due; there being one swamp in it . . . that contains about 10,000 worth of cypress-timber . . . but I can make little advantage of it till I can compass a good gang of Negroes; but God knows when that will be. . . . I desire you would be so kind to pay my coz [cousin] Singleton so much money of that in your hands as will furnish my mother, and the children with cloaths [clothes] and necessaries for their voyage hither; and what remains (if any) must go towards their passage. . . . You may observe by the contents of this letter that our necessities were very great and pressing; for sure I am, if strangers here had not done more for us than friends in England; we had all been starv'd ere this.

> church, town-house, and other public structures, an artillery ground for the exercise of the militia, and wharves for the convenience of their trade and shipping.[11]

After the reestablishment of Charles Town, the town grew very quickly in population and commerce. A huge influx of colonists arrived from England, and up until 1690 more than a substantial proportion of the population came from Barbados.

## The Influence of the Barbadians

The colonists who came from Barbados so controlled the earliest years in South Carolina that even after their population decreased after 1700, their cultural imprint still wielded immense influence on the political and economic affairs of the colony. Typically Barbadian colonists were aggressive, wealthy, and primarily engaged in pursuing self-interests. One early local historian, Alexander Hewatt, described them as "bold adventurers, who improved every hour for advancing their interest, and could bear no restraints which had the least tendency to defeat their favourite views and designs."[12] Economic opportunity was, after all, the reason most of them came to Carolina in the first place. They were tough, experienced colonists who knew what it took to succeed on the frontier. Moreover, their willingness to commit illegal acts to get what they wanted served to escalate conflict with the proprietors.

## The Fundamental Constitutions

The conflict erupted almost from the beginning, when the proprietors decided to develop a government with a more structured framework to help the colonists cooperate and succeed at establishing the colony of Carolina. The document detailing this governmental model, called the Fundamental Constitutions, was first developed in 1669 primarily by one of the proprietors, Anthony Ashley Cooper (who became Lord Shaftesbury in 1672), and his secretary, John Locke.

Although the arrangements Cooper and Locke described were meant to bring greater justice and equality among citizens of the colony, the Fundamental Constitutions document was never adopted and put into practice, mainly because the level of involvement the government would take in people's lives made it impossible to implement. Over the course of almost thirty years it was revised five times, but none of the revisions was ever accepted and adopted by the colonists, who viewed the constitutions as an attempt by the proprietors to tighten control on colonial life in South Carolina. Over time these suspicions developed into serious disagreements between the colonists and the proprietors.

## Conflicts Between Colonists and Proprietors

Almost from the beginning, the colonists had created headaches for the proprietors through illegal or unfair trade practices. The earliest trade issue to create conflict between the colonists and the proprietors was that of the Indian trade.

The Indian trade in South Carolina was dominated by deerskin, which was made into leather, a high-demand item in England. For men who had the capital to invest in the necessary trade items, the Indian trade was a gold mine, as trader John Lawson remarked in

Deerskin dominated the trade between the natives and South Carolinians.

1709: "[Indian traders] soonest rais'd themselves [financially] of any People I have known in Carolina."[13] In 1699 South Carolina exported 64,000 deerskins; just seven years later this figure had jumped to over 121,000.

Such figures made the Indian trade lucrative to a large number of South Carolinians. However, Indian traders often used alcohol and intimidation to cheat Indians out of a fair trade, thereby increasing profit margins. Such practices often prompted Indians to retaliate by robbing or killing the traders. The proprietors, angered by the colonists' mistreatment of the Indians, hoped to prevent further unfair dealings by creating a monopoly on the Indian trade. They did this by paying some Carolina tribes, such as the Westo, more than the colonists did. This lasted only a short while, however, as the colonists became angry over the monopoly and persuaded the Cherokee to help them make war on the tribes participating in the monopoly. The Cherokee and the colonists virtually wiped out the Westo and other small tribes, breaking the proprietors' monopoly on the Indian trade.

An even more worrisome issue to the proprietors was the illegal trade of Indian slaves. Although the Indian slave trade occurred in several colonies, it was a major economic enterprise only in South Carolina. The proprietors placed temporary laws against it, such as this one: "Noe Indian upon any occasion or pretense whatsoever is to be made a Slave, or without his owne consent be carried out of our Country."[14] Nevertheless, colonists persisted in this trade so that by 1710, about twelve thousand Indians had been forced into slavery in England's Caribbean island colonies, and another fifteen hundred worked as slaves in South Carolina.

The proprietors condemned the Indian slave trade because they feared it would escalate violence between the natives and the colonists. South Carolina was ill equipped to defend itself against more populous Indian nations, and the proprietors wished to protect the colony by preventing war. But by 1715 the slave trade, combined with the continual unfair trade deals the colonists made with the Indians, incited a regional revolt among the Indians that became known as the Yamasee War.

Many Native Americans in South Carolina were forced into slavery even though it was against the law.

## End of Proprietary Period

The colonists were the victors of the Yamasee War, but at a cost in loss of lives and property that brought the issue of the colony's defense into the limelight. The colonists wanted the proprietors to provide more military protection from Indians, but the proprietors believed the best way to protect South Carolina was by getting the colonists to obey the laws. The proprietors thought that the colonists had brought the Yamasee War on themselves by not adhering to legal trade practices with the Indians.

The colonists continued to cause problems for the proprietary government for another reason, as well—one that was not the settlers' fault. Because of the colony's close proximity to French-controlled regions in the Mississippi Valley to the east, protection of the colony from invasion by the French or French-allied Indians

## The Yamasee War

*By 1715 the unfair practices of Indian traders in South Carolina had driven the various tribes of the region to the point of rebellion. Cheated, physically abused, and often forced into slavery, the Yamasee persuaded the Creek, Catawba, and other tribes to form an alliance against the European settlers.*

*Although rumor of a conspiracy to wipe out the South Carolina settlements spread in Charles Town, no one paid it much attention. However, on April 15, 1715, the Yamasee attacked several homes near Port Royal, killing nearly one hundred settlers. By June about 90 percent of the white traders had been murdered. Almost no settlers were left outside of Charles Town, most having fled for the safety of the town.*

*Colonist Francis Yonge recounted the events of the Yamasee War, quoted in Elmer D. Johnson and Kathleen Lewis Sloan's book,* South Carolina: A Documentary Profile of the Palmetto State:

> After some years . . . dealing between the inhabitants and several nations of Indians, with whom they traded . . . the said Indians . . . agreed to destroy the whole settlement [of South Carolina], by murdering and cutting to pieces all the inhabitants. . . . In the year 1715, . . . most of the traders that were with them in their town; and going among the plantations, murdered all who could not fly from their cruelty, and burned their houses. The occasion of this conspiracy . . . was attributed to some ill usage they had received from the traders, who are not (generally) men of the best morals. . . . In this war near 400 of the inhabitants were destroyed, with many houses and slaves.

*Although the Yamasee were defeated and driven out of South Carolina, isolated raids by them and the Creek continued through 1716 and did not stop completely until 1720.*

was crucial. Moreover, the wealth of the colony and its importance as a source of naval stores made its defense an issue of national significance to England. When the colonists requested military aid from the proprietors, their request was turned over to the Crown, which noted, "If the Queen was at the Expence of protecting and relieving the Province, the Government thereof should be in the Crown."[15]

The lack of military protection finally led the colonists to overthrow the proprietary government in 1719. That year a great deal of unrest had grown among the colonists because of higher taxes and the proprietors' reorganization of the upper house without popular consent. As one unidentified colonist later noted, "The whole People in general [were] prejudic'd against the Lords Proprietors to such a degree, that it was grown almost dangerous to say any thing in their Favour."[16]

A revolt broke out when rumors were heard that the Spanish were planning to attack Charles Town. Although the rumor was true, the Spanish later changed their plan, and Charles Town was not attacked. However, the people of Charles Town did not know this and decided not to risk the security of their colony, uniting to form an association in which members promised to "support whatsoever should be done by their Representatives . . . in disengaging the Country from the Yoke and Burthen they labour'd under from the Proprietors."[17] After several attempts to regain control, the proprietary governor, Robert Johnson, backed down, and the Commons House assembled and appointed a new provisional governor and sent a request to England for a royal charter.

The royal charter, however, could not be issued as long as the proprietors owned the colony. As a result, South Carolina existed in a kind of political limbo for the next ten years, during which a series of provisional governors served. After years of negotiations, the proprietors sold their interests in the colony to the Crown in 1729, allowing South Carolina to officially become a royal colony. Thereafter the absence of the proprietary conflict and an economic boom helped to usher in a period of political and social harmony in South Carolina.

## Chapter Three

# Daily Life in Colonial South Carolina

For people in colonial South Carolina, pursuing the good life was of prime importance. The economic security of both the colony and its individual inhabitants was represented by property and wealth, which in turn were protected by deeply entrenched social, economic, and political systems.

Despite the differences in economic opportunity between the low country and the backcountry, records show that almost every free person in colonial South Carolina could at least make ends meet. Colonist James Glen attested to this in 1751, saying that about five thousand had "plenty of the good things of Life" while another five thousand had "some of the Conveniencys of Life" and ten thousand had "the Necessarys of Life."[18] These figures represented about 80 percent of the free population in South Carolina, and the rest, which numbered about five or six thousand, just barely got by.

## Government in the Royal Colony of South Carolina

The material wealth of South Carolina and its inhabitants helped establish political harmony in the colonial government, creating common economic bonds and eliminating political divisions among colonial leaders. Historian Robert M. Weir explains the reasons for this:

> Perhaps the most important underlying factor was increasing prosperity which . . . knit the community together in several ways. It not only lessened competition among groups . . . but also fostered upward social mobility by individuals. This mobility, in turn, tended to homogenize [make the same] interest groups as successful merchants purchased plantations and in the process acquired an understanding of the planters' economic interests and problems. . . . By the end of the colonial period almost all of the prominent leaders among the professional men and merchants in the assembly owned plantations.[19]

A tranquil view of Charles Town before the Revolution.

Such shared interests led South Carolinians to develop a common body of political beliefs. The foundation of these beliefs was a distrust of human nature based on the observation that human beings were influenced by self-interest. In this view, government existed only to protect individual freedoms and property from the control of factions or individuals motivated by self-interest. Therefore, the people had a duty to resist any government that failed to protect these freedoms. Moreover, checks were instituted on the government to prevent one branch of the government from controlling the others.

The individuals to whom the responsibilities of government were entrusted were usually aristocratic planters. Wealth was assumed to have built the qualities of independence, courage, and virtue in a person, and the flourishing of economic ventures implied that the successful person was intelligent. The belief was that the possession of material things fostered rational behavior. Moreover, wealth enabled a person to get a superior education, which was thought to build political ability. Finally, the prestige of a rich person in public office helped gain popular respect for the government.

Accordingly, about two-thirds of the twenty to thirty seats of the elected assembly, called the Commons House, were held by wealthy low country planters. To meet the requirements for elected office, a person had to own five hundred acres of land plus ten slaves or other property worth £1,000, which is roughly equal to $25,000 today. The South Carolina Commons House was one of the most powerful assemblies of any of the American colonies because of the wealth of its members, many of whom had political connections with British officials in London. Thus the authority of the Commons House often influenced the actions of the governor and the twelve-member Council, the upper house of the legislature that also served as an advisory body to the governor. As in all the royal colonies, the governor and the Council members were appointed by the Crown.

The power of the Commons House over the governor and Council was further strengthened by great public support for elected officials who were "the representatives of the people . . . elected by them as the house of commons in Great Britain, to be the guardians of their lives, liberties, and properties."[20] The support

# Women in Colonial South Carolina

*Wealth and marriage dictated the role of women in colonial South Carolina. Women were an important channel through which property and money could be distributed, since in South Carolina both sons and daughters could inherit equally. Marriage was often a financial arrangement made by a couple's parents in which one powerful family formed an alliance with another.*

*However, marriage often left women with little control over their lives. Legally a married woman's property belonged to her husband. She could not own property or a business in her own name without her husband's consent. Nevertheless, either by choice or necessity, some women were well informed about their husbands' financial and business matters.*

*Unmarried or widowed women were free to own property and operate a business in their own name. The most common types of businesses owned by women were millinery shops, inns, and taverns, but some also owned nontraditional businesses. Usually this occurred because of a husband's death. Elizabeth Timothy, for example, took over her late husband's job as editor and publisher of the* South Carolina Gazette.

*Nevertheless, many women tended to remarry after the death of a spouse, returning to a life where their prime responsibility was assisting their husbands in their endeavors. Historian Walter Edgar gives evidence of this custom in his book,* South Carolina: A History:

> When describing their wives, some colonial South Carolina males sometimes used terminology that gives us an idea about the status of women. For his wife, [Robert] Pringle had "the most Tender Regard & Affection, as she makes me happy. . . . She is . . . naturally of a very Good Temper & Disposition." Upon the death of Eleanor Ball Laurens, Henry . . . remembered her fondly as "a tender and watchful mother and faithful bosom Friend, a Wife whose constant Study was to make me happy."

was immense because voting rights were granted to every white male who owned at least fifty acres, and nearly every white male in South Carolina did. In fact, many owned a great deal more than fifty acres, since South Carolina was the wealthiest colony in British North America. Ever since the end of the proprietary government, South Carolinians had been increasingly successful in their pursuit of wealth.

## Work and the Colonial Economy in South Carolina

Part of what made South Carolinians successful was that whenever the economy took a turn for the worse, the colonists found another way to make money and keep it going.

This is what happened near the turn of the eighteenth century when conflict with the Indians began to escalate, causing the deerskin trade to founder. Many former Indian traders turned to harvesting pitch and tar from the vast pine forests of South Carolina, which were made into stores used for waterproofing ships, ropes, and other naval items.

Naval stores were vital to maintaining England's naval defense, and England paid a large bounty (reward for doing something) for those produced in the colonies. During Queen Anne's War (1702–1713), the need for naval stores created an economic boom in South Carolina, which lasted beyond the war because of an extension of the bounty. Between 1713, when the colony exported over six thousand barrels of tar, and 1719, when more than fifty-two thousand were exported, the production of naval stores increased by 800 percent.

The boom from naval stores lasted until 1724, when England required that tar and pitch be produced in the Swedish method to earn the bounty. The Swedes cut down green trees from which the tar and pitch were rendered, while South Carolinians used trees that were already fallen. Using trees that were already fallen allowed colonists to save labor by not having to fell trees, which might require twenty to be cut before one with a high amount of resin (the tree sap from which tar and pitch were made) was found. This labor-saving technique allowed the colonists to turn a high profit, so when the bounty requirements changed, many South Carolinians turned to producing a different commodity.

## From Naval Stores to Rice and Other Staples

The commodity was rice, which had been produced in the colony for many years but did not become a staple crop until the 1720s. Rice became the prime export of South Carolina, although it was produced mostly in the low country because rice fields had to be cultivated in swamps, most of which were along the coastline. In the 1720s, rice planters earned profits of 16 to 25 percent, although some of the more able planters reaped profits as high as 33 percent. Profits such as these motivated increased numbers of planters to invest in rice, often called "Carolina gold." By the 1740s, rice exports had grown from 6 million pounds annually to 30 million pounds in just twenty years.

In the backcountry, the lack of swampland prevented farmers from cultivating large rice fields and growing rich off the profits. Rather, various other crops were grown. A newspaper article dispatched from Charles Town in November 1768 offered a glimpse of the backcountry produce:

> Since the beginning of this month, several large quantities of excellent tobacco, made in the back settlements, have

Slaves harvest rice, a prominent and profitable staple crop.

been brought to this market. . . . The quantity of hemp made last year is nearly doubled this; [economic improvement has been so great] that the inhabitants now manufacture most of their linens . . . linsey-woolsey, and

## Rice Production

*Swamps were usually dammed so as to control flooding and then cleared of trees, brush, and other plants before a rice field could be planted. Historian Henry Savage Jr. described the cultivation of rice in his book* The Santee. *This excerpt is taken from* Perspectives in South Carolina History, *edited by Ernest M. Lander Jr. and Robert K. Ackerman:*

> First the meandering stream through the field must, by backbreaking digging with mattocks and shovels, be converted into a straight . . . canal. Around the whole field a lesser canal would have to be dug and the excavated earth spread evenly over the fields. Between these there would . . . be a grid of smaller ditches . . . to provide drainage, irrigation or flooding as needed. . . . [At] rice planting time . . . the selected seeds are dropped and lightly covered. To stimulate sprouting, kill . . . weeds and protect the seeds from the birds, the field is flooded for a few days [and then drained]. . . . Growth is stimulated and the crop protected by hoeing and periodic flooding, through the growing season. Finally, as the long, hot summer draws to a close . . . [there is] a waving golden sea of ripened grain. . . . Singing bands of brightly clad slaves, men and women, swinging shining hooks, cut and stack the harvest. From the field to the threshing shed go the laden carts, carrying in the cut of the previous day. In the shed, through the long, hot day, the most powerful of the slaves, with long flails, beat the golden grain from the straw. Through the fall and into the winter in wooden mortars the husks will be pounded from the kernels, the most tedious task of all. Finally, one winter day, several oversize dugouts will . . . take aboard their golden cargo—to be poled downstream and through the back waters to Charles Town [where it was shipped to England or the West Indies].

The indigo plant, one of the most common crops grown in South Carolina.

> even coarse cloths: that it has been proposed shortly to establish a stocking manufactory amongst them; that saw-mills are erecting in various parts; and the produce of good wheat has been so great this year that we may soon expect, from Camden alone, 2,000 barrels of flour and 1,500 of ship bread.[21]

Wheat, indigo, hemp, and tobacco were the most common crops grown in the backcountry. A backcountry farmer could do very well planting hemp and indigo, the most profitable crops, averaging the modern equivalent of about $30,000 a year. Some inland towns, such as Camden and Ninety-Six, turned to other enterprises, thriving on sawmill and gristmill operations. Georgetown built a small port that shipped about 5 percent of the colony's exports, while Beaufort, also a port town, shipped an equally small proportion of the total exports. Beaufort, however, became a major shipbuilding town in the 1760s because of the ample supply of live oaks on the nearby islands off the Carolina coast.

Indigo was the one crop farmers in both the low country and backcountry produced. Indigo became a staple crop when England became embroiled in war with Spain during the mid-1740s, causing rice prices to drop and making rice a "Verry dull Commodity all over Europe & America."[22] The stagnation of the rice crop led some planters to invest in a different crop. This crop was indigo, made popular in South Carolina by a teenage girl named Eliza Lucas (who would later marry into the prominent Pinckney family). In 1739 Lucas planted seeds her father had sent her from the Caribbean, and after five years she was able to produce seventeen pounds of dye from the plants. After sharing her success with other planters, South Carolina was exporting 138,000 pounds of indigo by 1747.

Although rice later rebounded, during the French and Indian War of the 1750s and 1760s, indigo became a staple crop second only to rice because England could no longer purchase indigo to make the blue dye for its military uniforms from France, its former supplier. However, like rice, indigo production required an inexpensive labor force to be profitable. Wealthy low country planters already had this labor force in considerable numbers of slaves, while those in the backcountry had few slaves, or none. As a result, less indigo was produced in the backcountry than in the low country. Nevertheless, South Carolina's wealth was dependent on crops produced with slave labor, fueling the continued existence of slavery and the growth of large plantations in the colony.

## Growth of Slavery and Plantations

Rice and later indigo production led to the growth of the African slave population in South Carolina, since both were labor-intensive crops. The colonists needed a cheap labor force to turn a profit, as a Charles Town merchant noted in 1758: "Labour Comes very High & Dear, which makes the Planters only Apply Themselves to the

Planting and Raising those Commodities that will bring Them in a Certain and present Advantage & Profitt. The planting of Rice, Indigo, &c. Answers to Afford the Value of High Labour."[23] During the 1720s, nearly nine thousand slaves were imported from West Africa, where the native peoples had lived in rice-growing areas for generations. These slaves already knew how to clear swamps, irrigate rice fields, and preserve rice seeds during floods. They also knew how to harvest the rice using a stick to beat it from the stalks and to grind off the husks with a mortar and pestle.

The wealth of planters and the growth of slave labor led to the development of large working plantations in the low country, where the swamps were located. Most planters actually owned several plantations among which their slaves were divided. For example, planter Ralph Izard placed 10 slaves at his Charles Town house and 69 at his residence plantation in Burton; the remaining 263 were spread out among five other working plantations.

Slaves from Africa were brought to South Carolina to provide the labor needed to grow and harvest rice.

## Life as a Slave

On South Carolina plantations, black slaves worked within a task system, meaning they were assigned specific jobs—such as hoeing, planting seeds, or husking rice—to do each day, while others worked as cooks, housekeepers, or nannies in the houses of their owners. When the daily work was completed, they could spend the rest of their day however they chose. Often they worked on their own dwellings, which they built themselves. Slave quarters were usually small wattle and daub (twigs and clay) or clay brick structures with thatched roofs. Many also spent this time working in their own gardens, fishing, or visiting relatives on nearby plantations. Although slaves were required to have a pass from their owners to leave a plantation, such passes were commonly granted during colonial times.

Most slaves did not work on Sundays and either visited family and friends or spent the day in Charles Town. Although laws were passed forbidding taverns to serve alcohol to slaves without the permission of their owners, the laws were usually ignored. Thus many slaves gathered in town on the Sabbath to drink and play games such as pitch-penny, pawpaw, and huzzle-cap. Historians believe that slaves were allowed this free time so that the colonists could preserve the "good order and the harmony of the whole community."[24]

Not all slave owners shared the idea that keeping the slaves content was good for the community. Many slaves were punished harshly for anything from not completing a task to talking back to an overseer [supervisor]. Punishments were usually in the form of whippings, but serious offenses met with mutilation or death. In 1740 a young slave woman named Esther was sent to Portugal, away from her family and friends, by her owner Robert Pringle, simply because he tired of her regularly leaving the plantation to visit her parents. Some slaves ran away, making it to Spanish Florida if they were not caught, although runaways represented only about 1 percent of the total slave population in colonial South Carolina.

## Education in Colonial South Carolina

Few slaves were taught to read and write unless they had an unusually benevolent owner. Such accomplishments were not considered necessary for the kinds of work most slaves did. Similarly among the free inhabitants of colonial South Carolina, educational opportunities were limited for most girls and many boys. If parents could read and write, they taught their children at home. Some sent their children to one of the local parish schools, though such schools were few and often too far away for many rural children to attend. Sons of artisans or modest farmers were expected to get a practical rather than classical education. This meant they learned primarily basic reading and simple arithmetic to enable them to take over the family business or farm. Others were apprenticed between the ages of twelve and fourteen to an artisan for a period usually lasting four years, during which they learned a craft such as upholstery, blacksmithing, wheel making, or tailoring. Education for girls was intended primarily to foster charming manners and conversational abilities, a pursuit usually limited to the daughters of well-to-do families.

The wealthy either hired private tutors or sent their children to one of the schools in Charles Town, the educational center of the colony. Colonial leader William Bull remarked that Charles Town offered "teachers of mathematics, arithmetic, fencing, French, drawing, dancing, music and needlework, to fit men for the busy world, and ladies for the domestic social duties of life."[25]

Higher education was an option only for the wealthiest families. Since there were no colleges in South Carolina, young men usually attended one of the institutions in the North or were sent abroad. By the 1770s, the South Carolina low country planters had more sons attending college in England than any other colony. This was partly because the cost of sending a son to college in Europe was so high that only the richest in the American colonies could afford it, and a good deal of these rich people resided in South Carolina. Planter Henry Laurens complained about the "considerable Sums of Gold and Silver . . . remitted to pay for the Board and Education of our Children"[26] at a university in Geneva, but he had visited schools in New England and England and found them wanting.

## Religion in Colonial South Carolina

Just as education in South Carolina was minimal compared with that in the northern colonies, the moral restrictions of South Carolinians tended to be lax in comparison as well. In a colony where the pursuit of wealth was the primary goal, religion played a minor role. Church attendance was sporadic, and Sundays were frequently a day of sport for the men. This was more apparent in the backcountry, where the Reverend Charles Woodmason, an Anglican (Church of England) missionary, once preached a sermon on behaving properly in church, which included rules prohibiting the presence of dogs in church and the drinking of alcohol during sermons.

Although the official church of South Carolina was Anglican, the prevailing attitude was that salvation was more important than a particular doctrine, as reflected in a letter written by Dr. Charles Burnham, who employed a dissenter, or non-Anglican, when he could not find an Anglican clergyman to baptize his children, around 1720: "I don't dout [doubt] but they will git as sone [soon] to Heaven that way as the other."[27] After the 1720s, many Anglicans who had no rector available turned to clergymen from dissenting churches to get married or have their children baptized.

The variety in denominations was high, even in Charles Town where the dominant church was Anglican. An engineer of the town remarked in 1773 that the city had

> [two Anglican churches] . . . a Presbyterian, a french [Huguenot], a German [Lutheran] and two Baptists; there is also an assembly for Quakers, and another for Jews [that were different] in religious Principles, and in the Knowledge of Salvation [but were] far from being encouraged or even inclining to that Disorder which is so common among Men of contrary religious Sentiments in many other parts of the World.[28]

The low country planters attended church regularly because it gave them an opportunity to display their social position in the

Wealthy families of South Carolina wore their finest clothes to church to display their high social status in the community.

community. To this end, the wealthy families of South Carolina showed up for services decked out in their finest clothes, and afterward they often not only entertained other well-to-do families but also hosted a reception for those less fortunate.

Economic status gave aristocratic South Carolinians the power to control the government, allowing them in turn to protect their property. Because economic security and the protection of property were at the core of Carolinian political beliefs, the royal government's failure to help maintain the status quo was regarded as a serious wrong. The wealthy planters believed that they had a responsibility to oppose rule by the British monarch, not just for their own self-interests but to preserve the interests of all people of South Carolina.

★ ★ ★ ★ ★

## Chapter Four

# The Revolution: Property Rights Equal the Rights of Men

When British subjects in North America began to work toward achieving independence from England, South Carolina was not only one of the first colonies to join the movement but also one of the most enthusiastic. Believing that freedom was inextricably tied to property rights, wealthy South Carolinians of the low country concluded that to preserve their freedom, they must cease to be subject to a government that failed to respect and protect these rights. There was considerable opposition to this idea in the backcountry, mainly during the early years of the struggle for independence; as the British threat extended inland, however, many opponents changed their minds.

## The Stamp Act

In the middle of the eighteenth century, England began imposing a series of laws designed to tighten control over its North American colonies. After England fought and won the French and Indian War (1756–1763), the Crown decided that the colonies should help pay for the cost of the war. Thus Parliament passed legislation to force the colonies to contribute to this effort.

One new law was the Stamp Act of 1765, which required an official stamp to be purchased for playing cards, legal papers, and newspapers. Colonists in South Carolina opposed the act because it was passed by the British Parliament, in which they had no direct representation. They did not want to set a precedent by submitting to an act that put control of their property in the hands of a legislature in which they had no voice. One of South Carolina's leading radical assembly representatives, Christopher Gadsden, echoed this belief when he wrote that "the principal reason [of opposition against the act is] its inconsistency with that inherent right of every British subject, not to be taxed but by his own consent."[29]

In Charles Town the reaction to the Stamp Act was explosive. A newspaper account tells what happened the day after the stamps arrived in the port of Charles Town:

> Early this morning . . . appeared suspended on a gallows twenty feet high, an effigy designed to represent a [stamp] distributor . . . with a figure of the devil on its right hand, on his left a boat, with a head stuck upon it. . . . On the gallows . . . was written, "Liberty and No Stamp Act" and on the back . . . "Whoever shall dare attempt to pull down these effigies, had better been born with a millstone about his neck and cast into the sea. . . ."
>
> In the evening the figures were [carried] to the Bay, attended by at least two thousand souls . . . halting at the door of a house belonging to George Saxby [a suspected distributor]. . . . Some small injuries [occurred] to the windows . . . [but] no such papers [were] found . . . [and the demonstrators] proceeded to the green . . . [where] the

effigies were committed to the flames, amidst the loud and repeated shouts.... There was a most solemn knell [stroke of a bell] for the burial of a coffin on which was inscribed "American Liberty."[30]

Colonists burn papers containing British stamps to protest the passage of the Stamp Act.

The mob action frightened royal officials, who shut down the government rather than try to administer the stamps. Public offices, courts, and the Charles Town port were closed.

Although no stamps were ever sold in South Carolina, the closing of the Charles Town port and lack of stamps created a dire problem for the city. Merchant ships continued to land in the port, but could get no clearance to leave without the stamps. As a result, no rice exports left Charles Town for four months, which was a blow to the colony's economy. Moreover, the presence of hundreds of idle sailors caused an increase in crime in the city. Finally, some ships gained clearance with stamps from Georgia, while others were issued certificates stating that no stamps were available, allowing the sailors and the rice to leave the port.

In 1766 the Crown repealed the Stamp Act. Gadsden, however, warned his fellow South Carolinians that the tension with England was far from over: "That province [colony] that endeavors to act separately will certainly gain nothing by it. There ought to be no New England men, no New Yorker, etc., known on the Continent, but all of us Americans."[31]

## The Townshend Acts

Gadsden's suspicions turned out to be justified, as Parliament soon followed the repeal of the Stamp Act with the Townshend Acts of 1767, which taxed glass, lead, paint, paper, and tea. South Carolinians protested these acts as they had the Stamp Act, and many planters and artisans agreed to boycott all taxed goods. Merchants, however, did not want to stop importation of these goods, believing it would damage business. This disagreement led many planters and artisans to threaten to stop business with any merchant who purchased the taxed goods.

Finally, the three factions met and worked out a compromise: no slaves and most British manufactured goods were to be imported, with the exceptions of writing paper, hardware, and cloth used for slave clothing. The Sons of Liberty, a group of politically radical colonists, enforced the compromise by openly harassing merchants who failed to comply with it. Once the nonimportation agreement went into effect, British imports dropped by more than 50 percent.

In response, the Crown repealed the Townshend Acts but retained the tax on tea as a reminder to the colonies that the Crown still had the power to tax them. In 1770 South Carolinians

## Life in British-Occupied Charles Town in the 1780s

*Eliza Lucas Pinckney described her troubles in British-occupied Charles Town, where she had gone during the war for safety, in her journal, quoted here from Elmer D. Johnson and Kathleen Lewis Sloan's book,* South Carolina: A Documentary Profile of the Palmetto State:

> After the many losses I have met with, for the last three or four desolating years from fire and plunder . . . I still had something to subsist upon, but alas the hand of power has deprived me of the greatest part of that, and accident the rest. . . .
>
> The labor of the slaves I had working at my son Charles' [Cotesworth] . . . estate . . . has not produced one farthing since the fall of Charles Town. Between thirty and forty head of tame cattle, which I had on the same plantation . . . was taken last November for the use of the [British] army, for which I received nothing.
>
> My house in Ellory Street . . . which I . . . rented at one hundred per annum sterling, was in a short time after filled with Hessians, to the great detriment of the house and annoyance of the tenant, who would pay me no more for the time he was in it, than twelve guineas. I applied to a Board of Field Officers . . . [who] gave it as their opinion that I ought to be paid for the time it had been . . . in the service of Government. . . . I applied . . . for payment, but received nothing. . . .
>
> My plantation up the path which I hired to Mr. Simpson for fifty guineas the last year . . . was taken out of his possession and I am told Major Frayser now has it for the use of the Cavalry, and Mr. Simpson does not seem inclined to pay me for the last half year. . . .
>
> To my regret . . . the wood has also been all cut down for the use of the garrison, for which I have not got a penny.

Colonists dump tea from ships of the East India Company into the Boston Harbor in an event that became known as the Boston Tea Party.

decided to discontinue nonimportation of all previously taxed goods, except tea. Planter and lawyer Henry Laurens wrote in 1774:

> I commend the proceeding at [Charles Town] . . . the people will not purchase the commodity [tea]; it must remain in store and perish or be returned at the expense of those who sent it. There is a constitutional [inborn]

stubbornness in such conduct which must be approved of by every true Englishman, and open the understanding of those [the Crown] whose stubborn attempts to ensnare America are supported by no other plea than power.[32]

## Reaction to the Boston Port Bill

The boycott of tea continued until 1773, when the Sons of Liberty dumped tea from the East India Company into Boston Harbor (an event that became known as the Boston Tea Party). England punished the city with the Boston Port Bill, which closed Boston's port until the East India Company was reimbursed for the destroyed tea. The Boston Port Bill outraged colonists in South Carolina, who saw it as a violation of the rights of merchants whose property was being withheld from the port without discriminating between the innocent and the guilty.

South Carolinians also feared that the Charles Town port might be next. Henry Laurens said the port bill was a law designed to "Cram down . . . every Mandate which Ministers Shall think proper for keeping us in Subjection to the Task Master who Shall be put over us."[33]

This fear prompted South Carolinians to support participation in a general intercolonial congress, which had been called by Massachusetts and was scheduled to meet in September. Five delegates were chosen—Henry Middleton, a planter; brothers John and Edward Rutledge; Christopher Gadsden; and Thomas Lynch—and were given the authority to commit South Carolina to whatever the colonies decided at the congressional meeting.

Thomas Lynch was one of five delegates chosen to represent South Carolina at an intercolonial congress in Massachusetts.

## Role in the First Continental Congress

During the meeting of the First Continental Congress, the South Carolina delegation created a stir over the issue of trade embargoes. The congress decided to place an embargo against exports to England and English territories, but at that point all the South Carolina delegates, except Gadsden, threatened to walk out of the meeting. Well aware that South Carolina's economy depended on the exportation of staple crops, the delegates argued that they would not agree to the embargo unless their colony would be allowed to continue exporting rice and indigo. This was necessary, they declared, because earlier regulations from London forbade the shipping of rice and indigo outside the British Empire, leaving South Carolina with no foreign markets for these important crops.

Eventually a compromise was reached. Rice would be exempt from the embargo, but indigo shipments would have to cease. To placate indigo growers in South Carolina, the delegation suggested that rice planters give a third of their profits to them as compensation.

## The War Begins

The South Carolina delegation returned home to find that a meeting had been called for the election of a provincial government. In January 1775, the Provincial Congress convened in Charles Town, and for the next several months attempted to overthrow the royal government. Provincial officials intercepted royal mail and in April one official letter to the governor revealed that England intended to use military force against the colonies.

The Provincial Congress decided to prepare for the worst. In May unidentified colonists confiscated sixteen hundred pounds of gunpowder, eight hundred muskets, and two hundred cutlasses from colonial stores. That month word came of the skirmishes between Massachusetts militia and British troops at Lexington and Concord, and soon rumors spread that the British intended to incite slave rebellions and Indian attacks. In response, the Provincial Congress decided to organize three regiments of colonial troops totaling fifteen hundred men.

Those who openly resisted the efforts of the Provincial Congress were dealt with harshly. Some, such as planter William Wragg, were banished to their estates and later run out of the colony, while others were tried and executed for suspicion of plotting slave insurrections or aiding the British.

By June 1775, however, many more colonists had come to the conclusion that reasoning with England would not regain their rights, and they were ready to go beyond trade embargoes and pledge their lives to the defense of their rights as free people. Colonist David Ramsay's account of the beginning of the Revolutionary War reflects this change of philosophy:

> The actual commencement of hostilities . . . the increase of arbitrary impositions from a wicked and despotic ministry—and the dread of insurrections in the colonies—are causes sufficient to drive an oppressed people to the use of arms. We, therefore . . . shall be justified . . . in resisting force by force. . . . We will go forth, and be ready to sacrifice our lives and fortunes to secure her [South Carolina's] freedom and safety. This obligation to continue in full force until a reconciliation shall take place between Great Britain and America, upon constitutional principles—an event which we most ardently desire.[34]

As Tories—those who were loyal to England—were met with increasing hostilities, in September 1775 the last royal governor, William Campbell, fled from Charles Town.

## The Battle of Sullivans Island

Campbell pleaded with British authorities to send troops to take control of Charles Town, and in June 1776 they complied. However, the colonists had anticipated a British attack and were prepared. Colonel William Moultrie successfully defended the town from the palmetto-log fort on Sullivans Island at the entrance to the bay through which ships entered Charles Town. General Charles Lee, commander in chief of the American forces in the South, wrote an account of the battle in a report to General George Washington:

> The [British] Commodore thought proper . . . to attack our fort on Sullivans Island. . . . They immediately commenced the most furious fire that I ever heard or

Colonel William Moultrie protected Charles Town when he defended Sullivans Island against a British attack.

> saw. I confess I was in pain from the little confidence I reposed in our troops, the officers being all boys, and the men raw recruits. What augmented my anxiety was, that we had no bridge finished of retreat . . . [and] I knew our stock of ammunition was miserably low. . . . The cool courage they [the American troops] displayed astonished and enraptured me; for . . . I never experienced a hotter fire—twelve full hours of it was continued without intermission. . . . Those who lost their limbs deserted not their posts. . . . However, our works was so good and solid, that we lost but few—only ten killed on the spot, and twenty-two wounded. . . . The loss of the enemy . . . was very great.[35]

## The Early War Years

It would be four more years before another major battle was fought in South Carolina, but skirmishes in the backcountry became commonplace. During the summer of 1776, the Cherokee, incited by the British, began raiding frontier settlements. In response, both North and South Carolina combined regiments and marched through fifteen inches of snow during the winter of 1776–1777, attacking Cherokee villages and capturing backcountry Tories. The Snow Campaign, as it came to be called, defeated the Cherokee, who ceded all their remaining lands in South Carolina to the colony and silenced opposition to the Provincial Congress in the backcountry for a while. The Cherokee stayed out of the war from then on, while the Catawba joined the American side and helped to track down Tories.

In the meantime, news of the Declaration of Independence had reached Charles Town, whose inhabitants celebrated jubilantly. Now the colony was a sovereign state, and the Provincial Congress authorized the development of a new constitution in 1777. Elected president of the new state was John Rutledge, who presided in Charles Town. For a while business went on as usual in South Carolina, while news of the war's progress came from afar.

## The Fall of Charles Town

This all changed in 1778 after the British captured Savannah, Georgia. Now the enemy had a vantage point from the south. The situation began to look dire for the colonists, whose troops had been severely depleted during a failed attempt to retake Savannah in 1779. Requests for more troops were sent to General Washington, who could manage to scrape together only a portion of the number required. Fearing an attack on Charles Town, the commander of the southern forces, Benjamin Lincoln, decided to move the army into the city.

This move proved to be a grave tactical error; the army became trapped on the peninsula between the Ashley and Cooper Rivers. This error made capture of the town that much easier for the British, who began a land siege and a naval blockade of Charles Town in March 1780. The siege lasted for two months, during

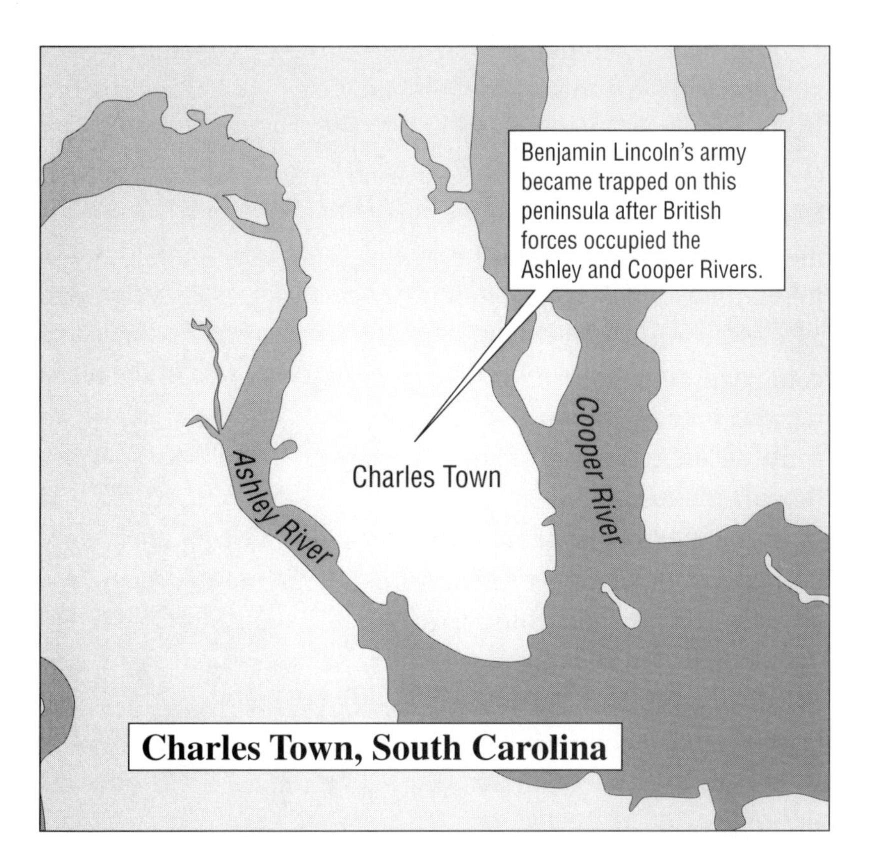


Charles Town, South Carolina

which the army's supplies and food dwindled. General Moultrie recorded the hardships in a journal:

> THURSDAY, 13TH: . . .The cannonade and bombardment continued, with short intermissions, until midnight. . . . Some women and children killed in town . . . [and] two houses were burnt. . . .
> THURSDAY, 4TH: Our [daily] rations of meat reduced to six ounces; coffee and sugar allowed only to the soldiers. . . .
> MONDAY, 8TH: . . .the remains of our cavalry were cut to pieces the day before yesterday. Our meat quite out; rice, sugar and coffee served out.
> FRIDAY, 12TH: . . . the fire was incessant almost the whole night; cannon balls whizzing and shells hissing continually amongst us . . . wounded men groaning along the lines. It was a dreadful night. It was our last great effort but it availed us nothing. . . . On the morning of the12th we marched out and gave up the town.[36]

Over fifty-five hundred American soldiers surrendered to the British that day. Governor John Rutledge had escaped to an obscure site in the backcountry in mid-April, allowing the state government to continue functioning even though the British, with the capture of Camden in August, had virtually taken control of all of South Carolina.

Sir Henry Clinton forced South Carolinians to take an oath that stated they would defend England against other colonists.

As they had in Georgia, the British in South Carolina began a campaign to win over the former colonists to the side of England, believing that

Tory sentiment was high in the South. However, the treatment the people of Charles Town received under the authority of British commanding officer Sir Henry Clinton persuaded many to do just the opposite.

The terms of surrender stated that Americans would not be mistreated as long as they agreed not to take up arms against the British. Yet Clinton forced South Carolinians to swear an oath of allegiance "that whenever I shall be thereunto required, I will be ready to maintain and defend the same [the British] against all persons whatsoever."[37] This meant that they would be forced to take up arms against their countrymen if they took the oath. Moreover, Clinton looked the other way when his army confiscated the estates of Whigs, as the American patriots were called, and wreaked destruction on many communities near Charles Town.

Clinton's worst blunder, however, was leaving Lord Charles Cornwallis in command at Charles Town when he left to join British forces in New York. Under Cornwallis several Whigs were executed, non-Anglican churches were burned, and the townspeople regularly abused. But when Cornwallis burned the home of Thomas Sumter, a militia officer and successful businessman, he committed an act that was to eventually cost the British their control of South Carolina.

## Rise of the Backcountry Militia

Sumter was so fiercely angered by the destruction of his home that he organized a resistance force in the backcountry in the summer of 1780. It was Sumter's spirited cry of retaliation that kept the American cause alive in South Carolina after the capture of Charles Town. Prior to 1780 many backcountry farmers had remained loyal to the British, but after they began to suffer abuse under them, many Tories changed sides. Within a year nearly all the backcountry had taken up arms against the British.

Using mostly guerrilla tactics, Sumter successfully raided British supply lines and led attacks against British troops. He also encouraged the leadership of other backcountry militia leaders, such as Francis Marion in the northeast part of the state. In fact Marion became even more feared than Sumter; as British officer Banastre Tarleton said, "Come let us go back and we will find the gamecock [Sumter]. But as for this damned fox [Marion], the devil himself could not catch him!"[38]

## Revolutionary War Heroes of South Carolina

Many unsung heroes in South Carolina sacrificed their lives and fortunes for the American cause, but perhaps the greatest is General Nathanael Greene. Although Greene never actually won a battle in South Carolina, recent historians have acknowledged his role in bringing the Revolution to its successful end. At the beginning of 1781, the British held all of South Carolina, but by the end of the year, they had been pushed back to Charles Town, largely as a result of guerrilla warfare in the backcountry. Historians believe that without the cooperation and support of the Continental forces, the guerrilla operations would not have been successful. It was Nathanael Greene who consistently communicated with guerrilla leaders and planned his attacks with the guerrillas.

The leading guerrilla fighter, Francis Marion, known as the Swamp Fox, became a popular folk hero after the war. At first his rough band of backcountry men was a source of amusement for the Continental troops. They soon proved their worth, however, as they ambushed British detachments and became a major source of interruptions in British military communications. Marion was successful because of the guerrilla tactics he used, such as attacking and immediately disappearing into the swamps. The enemy never knew from which direction his men would come; often they would give the impression of coming from the east, but then attacked from the west.

Women, as well as men, became known heroes of the war in South Carolina. Perhaps the most famous story was that of Rebecca Brewton Motte, who handed Marion a bow and arrow so his men could set fire to her own home, rather than let it fall into the hands of the British.

That the backcountry was in the control of the American guerrilla fighters became apparent to the British after the Battle of Kings Mountain on October 7, 1780. Here Major Patrick Ferguson took a stand against the hundreds of backcountry settlers from both North and South Carolina. When it was over, more than a

Francis Marion (left) was known as the Swamp Fox because of his cunning fighting tactics and ability to disappear into the swamps after attacking the British.

Thomas Sumter led the rise of the backcountry militia and persuaded many Tories to side with the colonists.

thousand British soldiers had been killed, wounded, or captured. This decisive victory proved to be a turning point in the war for Americans in South Carolina.

## The Tide Turns in Favor of the Americans

From this time on, the backcountry militia, aided by Continental troops under General Nathanael Greene, repeatedly skirmished with the British, gradually weakening their forces and driving them back toward Charles Town. The last major battle fought in South Carolina was at Eutaw Springs, on September 9, 1781. Historian David Ramsay provides an account of the aftermath:

> In the evening of the next day, [British] Lt. Col. Stewart destroyed a great quantity of his stores, abandoned the Eutaw, and moved toward Charlestown [Charles Town], leaving upwards of seventy of his wounded, and a thousand stand of arms. . . . The loss of the British amounted to upwards of eleven hundred men. That of the Americans was about five hundred, in which number were sixty officers.[39]

Although several battles were fought after Eutaw Springs, none were of much significance because the British had retreated to Charles Town, where they remained trapped until the war's end.

## The British Leave Charles Town

The British finally surrendered to the Americans at Yorktown, Virginia, in October 1781, but because peace negotiations dragged on, the British continued to occupy Charles Town for many months. Militia officer Peter Horry recounted the evacuation of Charles Town on December 14, 1782:

> The British offered to leave the town unhurt. Accordingly, at the firing of a signal gun in the morning . . . they quitted their advance works near the town gate, while the Americans, moving on close in the rear, followed them all along through the city down to the water's edge, where they embarked on board their three hundred ships.... In front [was the British] army, which . . . [had] captured our city, and . . . [whose soldiers had] hurled menaces and cruelties [toward the townspeople] disgraceful to the

> British name. And close in the rear, was our band of Patriots, bending forward with martial music and flying colors, to play the last joyful act of the drama of their country's deliverance. . . . Oh! It was a day of jubilee indeed; a day of rejoicing never to be forgotten. Smiles and tears were on every face.[40]

Now that Charles Town was back in the hands of Americans, South Carolinians set about the business of rebuilding their war-torn property, economy, and society.

Chapter Five

# The Postwar Years: Social and Political Upheaval

After years of enduring hardships from the war, South Carolinians were eager to regain their former prosperity and way of life. To celebrate their newfound independence from England, the residents of Charles Town renamed their city Charleston in 1783. Because their lifestyle depended on economic security, many South Carolinians were quick to forgive the British and return to doing business with them. As a result, retributions against Tories were less severe in South Carolina than in other states. The victors were willing to overlook past transgressions as long as business was good. However, this policy was resented in the backcountry, causing great political and social tension.

## Social Instability

The group primarily responsible for welcoming back the loyalists were the planters, the aristocratic elite who had depended heavily on the English market for the profits reaped from rice and indigo. Not everyone welcomed the British back with open arms, however.

In 1783 Charles Town was renamed Charleston in celebration of the colonies' independence from England.

In particular, the artisans and mechanics of Charleston and its vicinity resented the presence of the British, from whom they had suffered so many wrongs during the city's occupation and against whom many of them had fought.

The backcountry settlers were not happy about the easy acceptance of the British either, for these were the very people who had threatened their families and destroyed their farms. During the 1780s, however, the backcountry had a more pressing problem to deal with than the presence of loyalists in Charleston.

Soon after the end of the war, new settlers had swarmed into the backcountry, many of them outlaws and robbers. Travelers were frequently robbed and isolated farms ransacked. One backcountry settler, Judge Aedanus Burke, complained, "No man has security for even a worthless plow horse. . . . As to Trade and commerce it is at an end … unless the Government take some measures for extirpating [getting rid of] the outlyers [outlaws]."[41]

The state government was powerless to stop the violence, but did develop legislation designed to limit it. Eventually, in 1785, backcountry police—called rangers—were organized to help bring outlaws to justice and protect the settlers from further violence.

The chaos of the backcountry and the growing split between the planters and the artisan-mechanic faction in the low country were due largely to economic and political disorganization. Of the two disruptive forces, South Carolinians worried more about economics.

## Economic Changes

The war had left homes, farms, and mills burned all over the state, while fields lay abandoned and overgrown with weeds. A Port Royal minister described the destruction in postwar South Carolina:

> All was desolation. . . . Every field, every plantation, showed marks of ruin and devastation. Not a person was to be met with in the roads. All was Gloomy. [All society] seems to be at an end. Every person keeps close on his own plantation. Robberies and murders are often committed on the public roads. The people that remain have been peeled [stripped], pillaged, and plundered. Poverty, want, and hardship appear in almost every countenance.[42]

Not only did many South Carolinians have to rebuild their homes and farms, but they also had to replenish livestock that had been stolen or otherwise lost during the war. Moreover, the large planters needed labor to operate the rice and indigo plantations, and this required replacing the thirty thousand slaves that had either been taken or escaped during the war.

As a result, many South Carolinians sunk into massive debt to invest in new construction, livestock, and labor. Unfortunately, this investment proved difficult to pay off because of poor rice crops between 1783 and 1785. During these years, less than 50,000 barrels of rice were exported annually, a meager amount compared with the yearly average of 129,000 only a decade earlier. Moreover, by the early 1790s the indigo market was virtually

A colonial reenactment demonstrates how farms were salvaged after the Revolutionary War.

wiped out by competition from superior quality and less expensive indigo dye that Britain purchased from India.

As individual debts skyrocketed, the state attempted to foreclose on properties. Historian Walter Edgar describes how South Carolinians dealt with the threat to their property:

> Frightened and angry debtors thumbed their noses at the law. In 1784 in Camden, Hezekiah Maham, upon being served with a writ [a court-ordered written legal document], forced the sheriff's deputy to eat it and three others. The following year debtors closed Camden's courts to prevent foreclosures. In Cheraw . . . the people banded together to prevent sheriff's sales. Judge Aedanus Burke had all of his clothing stolen while on the circuit, and Judge Thomas Waties was pelted with mud and cow manure while on the way to open court. The most violent action took place in Winton (Barnwell) County, where the posted notices of sales were ripped down by a mob that later returned to trash the courthouse and set it afire.[43]

In an attempt to alleviate the social and economic problems in Charleston, the state government ordered Tories who had relocated from other states and those who had originally been on a banishment list, but never forced to leave, to remove themselves from South Carolina. With them went a major source of business, which angered the debt-ridden planters, but the state followed up the banishment order by allowing debtors to pay their creditors with land in place of cash. This relieved the debt of some individuals, while others were able to secure government loans to pay their debts. This strategy introduced currency into the economic system again and gave the economy a small jump start.

## Political Maneuvers

Although the economic strain affected both the low country and the backcountry, the low country planters continued to exercise more influence and power in the state government. Because they had fought so fiercely during the war while the low country planters had lived a relatively more peaceful life in occupied Charleston, those from the backcountry felt they deserved to have a greater say in state politics. This was backed up with the assertion that over 60 percent of South Carolina's population resided in the backcountry, and yet they continued to have only one representative for every six from the low country. Some of the more farsighted politicians thought this tension might be relieved if the capital were relocated to a site in the backcountry. In 1786 the government voted to move the capital from Charleston to a new town that was to be called Columbia.

These measures were attempts to restore harmony and peace in South Carolina so that the economy would have a chance to function properly. However, the state would have to muddle through the problems of the 1780s for a decade before resolving its economic and political tensions. Some of the farsighted politicians believed that the measures were temporary stays on chaos at best. These men thought that the national government ought to have more authority so as to take control during times of crisis. In its current state, the national government was nearly

Charles Pinckney's proposal to amend the Articles of Confederation brought national attention to the fact that the articles needed to be reformed.

powerless, its hands tied by the limits imposed by the Articles of Confederation, the forerunner to the U.S. Constitution.

One man, Charles Pinckney, a delegate to the Confederation Congress (as the national legislature was called then), organized a congressional committee that proposed seven amendments intended to strengthen the articles. Although the amendments were never considered, Pinckney's efforts were important in that they helped bring national attention to the need to reform the Articles of Confederation.

## The South Carolina Constitutional Convention Delegation

In 1787 a call for a constitutional convention to meet in Philadelphia in May was made. South Carolina chose five delegates, all planters and lawyers: Pierce Butler, Henry Laurens, Charles Pinckney and his cousin Charles Cotesworth Pinckney, and former governor John Rutledge (also a cousin of the Pinckneys). Thus the interests of the low country planter-elite faction were mainly presented in Philadelphia, to the disadvantage of the artisan-mechanic faction and the backcountry people.

Nevertheless, the South Carolina delegation was influential throughout the convention. Rutledge served on five committees and had a major input in the final draft of the Constitution. Charles Cotesworth Pinckney helped draft a compromise on the issues of the slave trade and navigation acts, both of which had considerable impact on South Carolina's economy. Charles Pinckney made over one hundred speeches and proposed the amendment to Article 6 that "no religious test shall ever be required as a qualification to any office or public trust under the authority of the United States."[44] Butler came up with the idea of having the Constitution take effect upon the ratification of at least nine states.

The prime objective of the South Carolina delegation was to create a strong national government that would not interfere in their state's economic aspirations. Because the issue of slavery was at the core of many of South Carolina's interests, it came up in many debates about congressional representation, navigation (trade) acts, taxation, and conditions for new states applying for admission to the Union.

## The Representation Debate

Rutledge led the delegation in supporting proportional representation (meaning the number of representatives allowed a state was based on the state's population) in both the House and the Senate because, like most southerners, he believed that in time South Carolina and the other southern states would grow sufficiently in population that they would eventually have a majority of representatives in Congress. South Carolina also wanted its slaves, who made up over 70 percent of the population in half its counties, to be considered state residents for purposes of determining the size of the state's congressional delegation.

The smaller states in the North opposed both proportional representation and the counting of slaves because with their smaller populations, they feared their interests would be swallowed up by those of the larger states. They also feared that if the South were allowed to count its slaves, then South Carolina and Georgia would import new slaves at a furious pace to increase their populations quickly.

Eventually a compromise was reached, allowing proportional representation in the House and equal representation in the Senate. However, the issue of whether to count slaves and, if so, how they were to be counted, was still to be resolved. With the North adamantly opposed to counting slaves, South Carolina delegate Charles Cotesworth Pinckney asserted the stance of the South, saying that "property in slaves should not be exposed to danger under a government instituted for the protection of property."[45] In other words, the South would not accept a system under which slaves were not counted at all. By standing firm, South Carolina

## The Pinckneys of South Carolina

Perhaps the most distinguished family of colonial South Carolina was the Pinckneys. Eliza Lucas Pinckney was one of the most respected women of her time—when she died in 1793, George Washington asked to be one of her pallbearers. Born in 1722 in the West Indies, she was educated in England but moved to South Carolina in 1738 with her family. Soon after, her mother died and her father had to return to the West Indies, where he was a British military officer. At the age of sixteen, Eliza took charge of her father's plantations. She also read extensively and experimented with indigo, which later became a staple crop in South Carolina. After her marriage to Charles Pinckney, a former speaker of the Commons House, she had four children in whom she instilled a love of botany, agriculture, and public service.

Her eldest son, Charles Cotesworth Pinckney (1746–1825), was educated in England and studied chemistry, military science, and botany. Back in South Carolina he became a lawyer, but during the Revolution he served as a Continental army officer. He was an influential delegate to the Constitutional Convention and later served as minister to France in the Adams administration. He became a national hero in 1797 when he refused to take a bribe from a French agent, saying, "No! No! Not a sixpence!"

His cousin, Charles Pinckney (1757–1824), was a political maverick not only on the national level but also within the South Carolina political circle. He was also educated in England, but the Revolution prompted him to return home early. He subsequently served as a lieutenant in the South Carolina militia. After the war, he served as a confederation congressman and was one of the most influential delegates at the Constitutional Convention. Despite his intelligence and political talent, he was vain, ambitious, and manipulative and not well liked. However, he went on to serve four terms as governor of South Carolina, two as a U.S. senator, and one as a U.S. congressman. He was appointed minister to Spain in 1801.

hoped to ensure for itself a population high enough to warrant a sufficiently numerous representation in Congress to protect the continued existence of slavery.

Charles Cotesworth Pinckney wanted to ensure the existence of slavery by including slaves in South Carolina's census.

In the end, a compromise was reached. Slaves were to be counted as three-fifths of a person, with mandatory reapportionment every ten years to allow for regular recounting of the state populations and subsequent adjustment of the number of representatives. To ensure that South Carolina and the rest of the South did not import slaves solely to increase their populations, taxation was to be based on the number of representatives in Congress. Faced with higher taxes, the South would be less likely to import great numbers of slaves in a short period of time. This compromise, however, said nothing about slavery in the western lands claimed by the states.

## The Western Lands Debate

Some of the southern states held claims to western lands from their original grants that extended all the way to the Mississippi River. These lands were of great value to the new nation because of their rich soil, abundance of wild game and minerals, and the great natural transportation system the Mississippi River waterway offered. Settlers were flocking to the West in increasing numbers, lured by the prospect of cheap land. However, the difficulties of transportation and communication—it took a month to travel from the East Coast to the Mississippi—made it impossible for the governments of the eastern states to control the western lands. Moreover, the new settlers had come from all over the former colonial territory and felt little, if any, loyalty to the new state that claimed "their" land. Rather, these settlers wanted their regions to be admitted to the Union as separate states.

The issue of admitting additional states into the Union introduced the question of whether slavery would be permitted in the new states. Clearly the North wanted the new states to be free, but South Carolina and the rest of the South wanted them to accommodate the institution of slavery. However, most of the delegates at the convention realized that some northern states would be unlikely to ratify a constitution that both allowed the counting of slaves for census purposes and granted permission for slavery in the western lands. To protect the success of the convention, South Carolina and other southern delegations agreed to another compromise.

This time the South made a concession. Slavery was to be prohibited in any new states cut from the Northwest Territory (now the states of Ohio, Indiana, Illinois, Michigan, Wisconsin, and part of Minnesota). This territory consisted of the western lands north of the Ohio River that had formerly been claimed by some of the northern states but had been relinquished to the national government for sale for payment of war debts. In exchange, nothing was said about prohibiting slavery in the western lands south of the Ohio River (now the states of Kentucky, Tennessee, Alabama, and Mississippi). The absence of a ban on slavery was equivalent to permission, but since the matter was not spelled out in the Constitution, and since slavery was specifically prohibited in the Northwest Territory, antislavery states in the north were mollified. The slave trade, however, continued to be a hotly debated subject, and objections to its continuance would also be raised by some northern states when it came time for ratification.

## The Slave Trade–Export Tax Compromise

In supporting the continuance of the foreign slave trade, South Carolina and Georgia were almost alone. Even Virginia, a slave state, wanted the slave trade abolished. Some of the convention delegates proposed placing a time limit on the slave trade, but initially the South Carolina delegation flatly refused to accept this. Charles Cotesworth Pinckney warned that the South would never go along with a time limit. When some antislavery delegates stated that slavery went against revolutionary principles of liberty and that to protect such an institution in the Constitution was abominable,

## The Mystery of the Pinckney Plan

Only in recent years have historians recognized Charles Pinckney's contribution to the U.S. Constitution. At the Constitutional Convention in 1787, Pinckney presented a plan on which to base the new Constitution. The Pinckney Plan, as it came to be called, was, however, the main rival competing with James Madison's Virginia Plan. Although many elements of both plans are included in the body of the Constitution, Madison discredited the Pinckney Plan after Pinckney's death in 1824, saying that it was never considered by the convention.

Although Madison failed to record the details of the Pinckney Plan in his otherwise meticulously detailed notes from the convention, the notes of other delegates, such as Pennsylvanian James Wilson, furnished evidence that the Pinckney Plan not only existed, but was seriously considered by the delegates.

The Pinckney Plan was not full of original ideas, as Madison's Virginia Plan was, but it was well thought out and logically organized. Most of his ideas were borrowed from the Articles of Confederation and the Massachusetts and New York constitutions, all of which Pinckney credited. Although an exact copy of the plan has not been found, historians have pieced together some of it. Pinckney advocated an executive of a single person and a bicameral legislature that could veto state laws. Much of the language of the Pinckney Plan made its way into the Constitution, including the terms "president," "House," and "Senate." From his plan came the ideas that the House should have the power to impeach, that the legislature should have the power to coin money, and that the president should serve as commander in chief of the armed forces. At least twenty-one provisions in the Pinckney Plan appear in the federal Constitution.

Rutledge went so far as to threaten that "religion and humanity had nothing to do with this question. Interest alone is the governing principle with nations. The true question at present is whether the Southern states shall or shall not be parties to the union."[46]

Once again a compromise, accepted by both proponents and opponents of the slave trade, resolved the issue. Again the proposal to limit the time for the foreign slave trade was made, but it was followed by an assertion that if South Carolina wanted a prohibition of export taxes, then it would have to give up something in return. South Carolina was one of only two states that were entirely dependent on the exports of their own produce. Therefore, it was to the benefit of South Carolina if the interstate trade system was regulated by the national government, while individual states would be free of export restrictions. Finally, the South Carolina delegation agreed to accept the abolition of the foreign slave trade after twenty years (it was finally ended in 1808) in exchange for the prohibition of taxes on exports. In addition, imported slaves were to be taxed.

## Ratification of the Constitution

After the convention ended in September 1787, the South Carolina delegation returned home and worked to build public support for ratification of the new Constitution. However, once again, those from the backcountry felt left out of the proceedings when Charleston was chosen as the site for the ratification convention. Judge Burke, a backcountry opponent of ratification, later claimed that Charleston was chosen because in that city "there are not fifty inhabitants who are not friendly to it. The merchants and leading men kept open houses for the back and low country members during the whole time the Convention sat."[47]

Nevertheless, the opponents of ratification presented their concerns to the convention, objecting in particular to the authority given to Congress to abolish the foreign slave trade in 1808. However, each time an objection was made, Charles Pinckney and Rutledge offered a reasonable explanation.

In the end, the convention voted for ratification 149 to 73. Most of the votes in favor were from low country planters, merchants, and lawyers, and when ratification was announced, celebrations took place in Charleston and other low country areas. Among the backcountry delegates, however, more than half voted against ratification. Judge Burke, who claimed that 80 percent of backcountry settlers opposed the Constitution, described the events that took place in that region after ratification: "In some places the people had a coffin painted black, which, borne in funeral procession, was solemnly buried, as an emblem of the dissolution and interment of publick liberty."[48] South Carolina entered into the Union as the eighth state on May 23, 1788, in an atmosphere of deep social tensions.

John Rutledge was a major contributor to the final draft of the Constitution and advocated the idea of state representation on the basis of state population.

These social tensions were evident when the first elections for federal congressional representatives were held. Two of the five representatives were from the backcountry, and thereafter the low country elite could not exclusively control state interests in the federal Congress. For two decades, suspicion and hostility existed between the leaders of the two regions, who often referred to each other in derisive terms based on class. Historian Walter Edgar wrote that "they [low country elite] referred to backcountry [folks] as 'yahoos' and 'a parcel of illiterate second rate fellows' and those in the lowcountry [were referred to by the backcountry] as 'demagogues and blockheads.'"[49] By 1808, however, those from the low country realized that the state's political woes were getting out of hand. That year a compromise was made, and for the first time fair apportionment was implemented throughout South Carolina.

After the low country and backcountry established fair representation in South Carolina, the state entered a peaceful era known as the antebellum period.

Thereafter South Carolina entered into a half century of peaceful existence, known as the antebellum period, the era "before the war." The war, of course, was the Civil War. For peace had been bought at the expense of the liberty of more than half the state's population—the black slaves—and with the end of slavery would come the end of South Carolina's way of life. Nevertheless, today South Carolina is once again a prosperous state, where people can pursue the American dream of economic independence, fortified by a tradition of protecting the freedom and liberty that now extends to all South Carolinians.

# Notes

## Introduction: South Carolina's Wealth

1. Quoted in Christopher Collier and James Lincoln Collier, *Decision in Philadelphia: The Constitutional Convention of 1787.* New York: Ballantine Books, 1986, pp. 98–99.

## Chapter One: Before the Colony: The Struggle to Settle Carolina

2. Quoted in Elmer D. Johnson and Kathleen Lewis Sloan, eds., *South Carolina: A Documentary Profile of the Palmetto State.* Columbia: University of South Carolina Press, 1971, p. 29.
3. Quoted in Robert M. Weir, *Colonial South Carolina: A History.* Millwood, NY: KTO Press, 1983, p. 6.
4. Quoted in Johnson and Sloan, *South Carolina,* p. 8.
5. Quoted in Johnson and Sloan, *South Carolina,* p. 9.
6. Quoted in Walter Edgar, *South Carolina: A History.* Columbia: University of South Carolina Press, 1998, p. 30.
7. Quoted in Johnson and Sloan, *South Carolina,* p. 11.

## Chapter Two: Founding the Colony

8. Quoted in Johnson and Sloan, *South Carolina,* pp. 13–14.
9. Quoted in Spencer B. King Jr., *Georgia Voices: A Documentary History to 1872.* Athens: University of Georgia Press, 1966, pp. 2–3.
10. Quoted in Weir, *Colonial South Carolina,* p. 60.
11. Quoted in Johnson and Sloan, *South Carolina,* pp. 48–49.
12. Quoted in Weir, *Colonial South Carolina,* p. 61.
13. Quoted in Edgar, *South Carolina,* p. 135.
14. Quoted in Edgar, *South Carolina,* p. 136.
15. Quoted in Weir, *Colonial South Carolina,* p. 91.
16. Quoted in Weir, *Colonial South Carolina,* p. 101.
17. Quoted in Weir, *Colonial South Carolina,* p. 101.

## Chapter Three: Daily Life in Colonial South Carolina

18. Quoted in Edgar, *South Carolina,* p. 151.
19. Quoted in Weir, *Colonial South Carolina,* p. 122.

20. Quoted in Edgar, *South Carolina*, p. 117.
21. Quoted in H. Roy Merrens, *The Colonial South Carolina Scene: Contemporary Views, 1697–1774.* Columbia: University of South Carolina Press, 1977, p. 247.
22. Quoted in Edgar, *South Carolina*, p. 144.
23. Quoted in Edgar, *South Carolina*, p. 139.
24. Quoted in Edgar, *South Carolina*, p. 173.
25. Quoted in Edgar, *South Carolina*, p. 175.
26. Quoted in Edgar, *South Carolina*, p. 177.
27. Quoted in Edgar, *South Carolina*, p. 181.
28. Quoted in Weir, *Colonial South Carolina*, p. 220.

## Chapter Four: The Revolution: Property Rights Equal the Rights of Men

29. Quoted in Ernest M. Lander Jr. and Robert K. Ackerman, eds., *Perspectives in South Carolina History: The First Three Hundred Years.* Columbia: University of South Carolina Press, 1973, p. 63.
30. Quoted in Johnson and Sloan, *South Carolina*, pp. 157–58.
31. Quoted in Lander and Ackerman, *Perspectives in South Carolina History*, p. 64.
32. Quoted in Johnson and Sloan, *South Carolina*, p. 163.
33. Quoted in Weir, *Colonial South Carolina*, p. 313.
34. Quoted in Johnson and Sloan, *South Carolina*, p. 167.
35. Quoted in Johnson and Sloan, *South Carolina*, pp. 184–85.
36. Quoted in Johnson and Sloan, *South Carolina*, pp. 202–203.
37. Quoted in Edgar, *South Carolina*, p. 233.
38. Quoted in Edgar, *South Carolina*, p. 235.
39. Quoted in Johnson and Sloan, *South Carolina*, p. 224.
40. Quoted in Johnson and Sloan, *South Carolina*, pp. 225–26.

## Chapter Five: The Postwar Years: Social and Political Upheaval

41. Quoted in Edgar, *South Carolina*, p. 246.
42. Quoted in Weir, *Colonial South Carolina*, p. 336.
43. Edgar, *South Carolina*, p. 246.
44. Quoted in Edgar, *South Carolina*, p. 250.
45. Quoted in Collier and Collier, *Decision in Philadelphia*, p. 216.
46. Quoted in Collier and Collier, *Decision in Philadelphia*, p. 231.
47. Quoted in Edgar, *South Carolina*, p. 250.
48. Quoted in Edgar, *South Carolina*, p. 252.
49. Edgar, *South Carolina*, p. 254.

# Chronology

**1526**
First Spanish colony is settled by Lucas Vásquez de Ayllón near Georgetown and meets with disaster.

**1562**
French colony is established near Port Royal.

**1629**
King Charles I grants "Carolana" to Sir Robert Heath.

**1663**
King Charles II gives Heath grant to eight lords proprietors.

**1670**
English establish the first permanent settlement in South Carolina at Albemarle Point.

**1680**
Settlement is moved to Oyster Point and named Charles Town.

**1715**
Yamasee War erupts.

**1719**
Proprietary government is overthrown.

**1744**
Eliza Lucas (Pinckney) successfully produces dye from South Carolina indigo.

**1776**
British defeated during attempt to take Charles Town.

**1780**
March: British capture Charles Town.
October: Battle of Kings Mountain turns the tide in favor of the Americans in South Carolina.

**1782**
British evacuate Charles Town.

**1783**
Charles Town is renamed Charleston.

**1786**
State capital is moved to Columbia.

**1788**
South Carolina becomes the eighth state in the Union.

# For Further Reading


Tracy Barrett, *Growing Up in Colonial America.* Brookfield, CT: Millbrook Press, 1995. This book discusses education, training, and leisure activities for children growing up in the American colonies.

Ruth Dean and Melissa Thomson, *Life in the American Colonies.* San Diego, CA: Lucent Books, 1999. This comprehensive book covers topics such as daily life in the cities and rural areas of the colonies; typical employments; immigrants; changes in political, religious, and social attitudes; and relations with the Native Americans.

Bobbie Kalman, *Colonial Life.* New York: Crabtree, 1992. This book provides brief information and dramatized photographs about colonial homes and towns, family life, play and school for children, men's and women's fashions, travel, and life of a slave family.

Deborah Kent, *America the Beautiful: South Carolina.* Chicago: Childrens Press, 1990. This book offers information on the land, people, and culture of South Carolina. It includes a section with interesting anecdotes on colonial history.

Bonnie L. Lukes, *Colonial America.* San Diego, CA: Lucent Books, 2000. This book offers a comprehensive look at the development of the American colonies. It includes a chapter that covers the settlement and colonial history of South Carolina.

Marguerite Couturier Steedman, *The South Carolina Colony.* London: Crowell-Collier Press, 1970. This book includes chapters that focus on the Native Americans of the region, the Spanish settlements, the harsh conditions settlers endured, the Yamasee War, the rise of the backcountry, and the early revolutionary years.

R. Conrad Stein, *South Carolina.* Danbury, CT: Childrens Press, 1999. This book includes a brief section on the exploration and colonial history of South Carolina. It includes a gallery of famous people from the state, a map, and a historical time line.

# Works Consulted

Harry J. Carman, Harold C. Syrett, and Bernard W. Wishy, *A History of the American People: Volume I to 1877.* New York: Alfred A. Knopf, 1960. This comprehensive text offers in-depth information on the settlement of the colonies, the development of a colonial economy, intercolonial conflicts, and changes in the political and religious climate in colonial culture. It also discusses the process of creating the federal Constitution.

Christopher Collier and James Lincoln Collier, *Decision in Philadelphia: The Constitutional Convention of 1787.* New York: Ballantine Books, 1986. This book offers an in-depth look at the process by which the founding fathers developed the federal Constitution. It provides insight into the motivations of the individual delegates who framed the document and pieces together how these various factors contributed to the final work.

Walter Edgar, *South Carolina: A History.* Columbia: University of South Carolina Press, 1998. This book offers information on the Spanish era, the early colonization, the ethnic makeup of the settlers, the proprietary and royal governments, the economy, relations with the Native Americans, everyday life, the Revolution, and the disharmony of the postwar years. Interesting anecdotes support the text.

David Hawke, *The Colonial Experience.* New York: Bobbs-Merrill, 1966. This book provides a comprehensive look at the reasons for colonial settlement and also discusses the politics, society, economy, and religion of the colonies.

Elmer D. Johnson and Kathleen Lewis Sloan, eds., *South Carolina: A Documentary Profile of the Palmetto State.* Columbia: University of South Carolina Press, 1971. This book provides primary quotes from historical documents and personal letters and journals related to South Carolina history.

Paul Johnson, *A History of the American People.* New York: HarperCollins, 1997. This book offers an in-depth look at the early settlement and colonial era of the United States. It includes informative sections on colonial politics at all levels and the development of the colonies' independence from England.

Spencer B. King Jr., *Georgia Voices: A Documentary History to 1872.* Athens: University of Georgia Press, 1966. This book about Georgia offers information pertaining to South Carolina as well. Each section is supported with primary quotes relating to the subject.

Michael Kraus, *The United States to 1865.* Ann Arbor: University of Michigan Press, 1959. This book explores the motivations behind settlement of the colonies, with brief sections devoted to South Carolina, and the political and social changes of the mid-1700s that led to the War of Independence.

Ernest M. Lander Jr. and Robert K. Ackerman, eds., *Perspectives in South Carolina History: The First Three Hundred Years.* Columbia: University of South Carolina Press, 1973. This book is a collection of secondary source material from various experts on the subject of South Carolina history. The topics pertaining to the colonial period include why Carolina was granted to the proprietors, details on the Fundamental Constitutions, early settlement, how the colonists wrested power from the proprietors, the rice industry, and reactions to the Stamp Act.

H. Roy Merrens, *The Colonial South Carolina Scene: Contemporary Views, 1697–1774.* Columbia: University of South Carolina Press, 1977. This book is a compilation of primary source material, including personal and official letters, reports, interviews, and journal entries. The topics include immigration to South Carolina, travel and economics, and observations of the backcountry and the low country.

Robert M. Weir, *Colonial South Carolina: A History.* Millwood, NY: KTO Press, 1983. This comprehensive book provides in-depth information on the history of South Carolina prior to settlement, the Native Americans of the region, the transformation of the government from proprietary to royal, the economy, the society, and the Revolution. Special emphasis is devoted to the effect of slavery in the South Carolinian society and economy.

# Index

# Picture Credits

Cover photo: © North Wind Pictures
© Bettmann/CORBIS, 25, 26, 51
© 2000 N. Carter/North Wind Pictures, 20
Dictionary of American Portraits, Dover Publications, Inc., 76
© Hulton/Archive by Getty Images, 21, 45, 58, 61, 67, 83
Chris Jouan, 9, 63
National Portrait Gallery, Smithsonian Institution/Art Resource, 79
Brandy Noon, 69
© North Wind Pictures, 18, 29, 30, 35, 39, 43, 64
The Pierpont Morgan Library/Art Resource, 16
© Joseph Sohm; ChromoSohm Inc./CORBIS, 84
© Ted Spiegel/CORBIS, 74
© Stock Montage, Inc., 13, 33, 47, 54, 57, 68, 72

# About the Author

Christina M. Girod received her undergraduate degree from the University of California at Santa Barbara. She worked with speech- and language-impaired students and taught elementary school for six years in Denver, Colorado. She has written scores of short biographies as well as organizational and country profiles for educational multimedia materials. The topics she has covered include both historical and current sketches of politicians, humanitarians, environmentalists, and entertainers. She has also written several titles for Lucent Books, on subjects such as Native Americans, entertainers, Down's syndrome, and learning disabilities, as well as *Connecticut* and *Georgia*, also part of the Thirteen Colonies series. Girod lives in Santa Maria, California, with her husband, Jon Pierre, and daughter, Joni.